simply

JOSH

To Aspen Camp
School for the
Deaf

All the Best!

Joshua Dowling

simply

JOSH

TATE PUBLISHING *& Enterprises*

Published by Tate Publishing & Enterprises, LLC
127 E. Trade Center Terrace | Mustang, Oklahoma 73064 USA
1.888.361.9473 | www.tatepublishing.com

Tate Publishing is committed to excellence in the publishing industry. The company reflects the philosophy established by the founders, based on Psalm 68:11,
"The Lord gave the word and great was the company of those who published it."

Book design copyright © 2009 by Tate Publishing, LLC. All rights reserved.
Cover design by Amber Gulilat
Interior design by Joey Garrett
Photography by Brittany Castle (www.brittanycastle.com)

Published in the United States of America

ISBN: 978-1-60799-827-3
Biography & Autobiography / General
09.08.10

DEDICATION

This book is dedicated to the following people:

Mom
The best mother anybody could ever ask for.
You are my Rock of Gibraltar.

Dad
Thank you for your unwavering love and faith in me.
You are an extraordinary father.

Christina
Without you, I would not know
the joy of being a brother.
I love you, CJ.

Grandma
Grandma, you are an amazing person.
God has blessed me with an extraordinary angel.

The Peters Family
Thank you for your amazing support during all the years.
Without your help, I would have not
experienced many wonderful
things. Most of all, without you,
Dr. Peters, I would have not
had a beautiful smile.

The Cassells
Thanks, Granny, Poppy, Aunt Kim, Kirsten,
Trey, Uncle Ed, Aunt Nola, and many more!
You all are a fine example of a
strong, close-knit family that
stand by each other through the test of time.

And also—-

The Sanders Family
Love you guys: Julia, Henry, Crystal,
Helen, Phoebe and Jexa!

Eddie Baskeyfield of the Baskeyfield family
Thank you for being the father who
helped to bring me into the world.

To Tammy, Henry, Debbie, Amanda, Mikey
and everybody else, you guys are cool!

And this book is created in memory of:

William Baldwin
The warmest great-grandfather anybody would have ever met.

Terry Malone and Michael Freeburg
We, the Westmoore High School
class of 1997, miss you both.

Kristen Rogers
You were not only my sign lan-
guage interpreter, but a friend.
I miss you.

Brenda Keller
We the Gallaudet community will always remember you and your energetic smile on campus.
You were the Mom on campus that made
sure I had my mail and my meals.

Shelley "Siren" Beattie
You were always, on and off the screen,
a gladiator. I'll always remember
our times in Orlando, our letters, and our friendship. You were an inspiration to us all.

ACKNOWLEDGMENTS

Writing a book is not an easy thing, for the lack of a better phrase. The time, the effort, and the cohesiveness of a community and its people should be recognized when it comes to creating an acknowledgement. With that in mind, I would like to take some time and extend my deep appreciation to everybody who made a contribution to this book. These people are nothing short of extraordinary, kind, warm, giving, and simply fantastic.

Tate Publishing, LLC
Special thanks to the entire staff of Tate Publishing for having guided me through the entire process that has helped make this dream a reality. All of you have made this such a pleasant, educational experience, and I look forward to many more years of successful future projects.

The Elementary to High School Years
Thanks to the administrators, teachers, speech therapists, counselors, and sign language interpreters from Red Oak Elementary School, Brink Junior High School, and Westmoore High School, all located in Moore, Oklahoma. You all have given a specific contribution to the person I have become today. Thank you, everybody.

The College Years

A sense of deep appreciation for the administration, faculty, staff, students, friends, and family at Gallaudet University, the world's only liberal arts university for the Deaf and hard-of-hearing students, located in Washington, DC. Many of you have helped solidify my sense of identity as a Deaf person, and because of your advice and encouragement, I am where I am today. God bless you, Gallaudet University.

Circle of Friends

A special nod to a group of my closest friends (but not limited to):

Tara Echo Anderson
Mistey Villanueva
Daniel Dickens
Heidi Sills
Rachel DeAnne Hollis
Ashley Lowe
Lindsay Anne Ryan
Mindy Brightman
Selina English
Taye Akinola
Tami Lee Santimyer
Nathan Klewin
Alena Francis
Rita Ann DeBono
Shannon Kapp
Mistella Kneil-Haefner
Terence L. Davidson
Katherine "Kate" Hasting
-and-
Sylvie Soulier

TABLE OF CONTENTS

PREFACE

This story is for everyone. It is for every single person from all walks of life; it matters not if you are old or young, blind or Deaf, black or white, rich or poor, or anything else. It matters not if you love God or not. This story is about a person who had so many factors working against him, influences that threatened to rob him of the most precious gift of all: life.

This story is not about someone famous; instead, it is about a Deaf child who decided to take everything he had learned and make it work. This story is about someone who decided that enough was enough: enough discrimination, enough anxiety, enough insecurity, and enough confusion.

This is about a young boy who, with the guidance of God, found the beginning and the purpose of his existence. This story shows how the boy in the corner no longer felt the need to hide.

And most of all, this story is about how a little Deaf boy from the farms and suburbs of Oklahoma found the most difficult thing that anybody could ever obtain: true happiness and the love for himself.

This is a story of personal triumph and liberation.

"WELCOME TO
THE WORLD"

On a cold, windy afternoon of November 28, 1979, a shrill, loud cry rang throughout the halls of the maternity ward.

The cry of the newborn seemed strong yet peaceful after the long, painful screams of labor that had rattled the ward the entire morning.

The exhausted, worn-out body of the young teenage mother seemed insignificant as she held out her arms to hold and welcome her new son in this world. The nurse, with a joyous look on her face, handed the newborn to her. The mother took and held him ever so gently. Her eyes were puffy and bloodshot, and every single muscle in her body could no longer function well; she had labored a great deal throughout the cold morning.

This was her first child.

Through tears, she looked at her new child and could not speak for the longest time. The young father, who was also a teenager himself, stood beside and looked at the son with awe. As the newborn boy lie there, snug and warm in the blankets, the parents wondered what they would name him. They were not sure. Also, an unsure future stood out in front of them. How will they provide for this child? What decisions do they have to make? They were scared. And so young. Young and inexperienced. The baby was fussing with a good, healthy dose of strength, and his eyes studied the parents intently.

"I know what to name him," the mother said, sniffling between sobs.

"Yeah?" the father inquired.

Looking at the child, the mother smiled and whispered, "Hello, Joshua. Welcome to the world." She smiled at her newborn son.

I looked into my mother's eyes, and a tiny smile came across my fresh face.

The young parents looked to the outside through the cold, sterile window, acknowledging it was finally over, the laborious experience. The bare, great oak trees outside rustled underneath the cold, cloudy Oklahoman sky, as if they were responding with happiness at this new arrival.

In order to tell a story, you have to write about what you know.

And this is what I know: My name is Joshua, and I have been Deaf all my life.

This is my story.

"Oh my goodness! Oh! What a beautiful baby!" my grandmother cooed at me.

"Look at that boy. He has your smile, Diana!" my

aunt said to my mother, who was lying on the couch, still in recovery.

It was a few days later, and the matriarch of the family on my mother's side had come to see the new child. Several other family members had come as well.

Over the years, my grandmother would also become one of the biggest role models in my life. The same goes for my Aunt Julie; her advice and perspective on things have helped mold my life, and her friendship is perhaps one of the most unique out there.

I was welcomed into a family where the women were strong like steel magnolias, who were independent and took care of everything to the last detail. Over the years, the strength of the women in the family would sustain me throughout my darkest chapters of life. It also would shape the way I saw the world in general.

Each one of us has a source of strength, a source that remains constant throughout the years, through the ups and downs of our own individual lives, one that carries us and glues ourselves together in the crazy place we all know as the "real life," a source that never completely goes away. For me, the source of my strength is within my family. Perhaps they don't understand it completely, but as time has gone by, that source had become stronger and stronger. I could not imagine my life without my family.

How could I, after all those times they have been there for me? Especially when I lost my hearing.

"Eddie? Something's wrong with Josh. Something's not right. Get over here please!" Mommy said to my biological father. Her tone carried a hint of hysteria in it. He came across the small living room of the apartment. They had started out with a small apartment to begin a new life together.

Rubbing and soothing me, she looked at me.

I was crying and screaming nonstop. I had been doing that way for a few days. Her face was heavy and fraught with worry, the overpowering response of a new mother. Her eyes were scanning my body and face. She didn't know what to do, and she was in a state of anxiety. My fever was running high, at about 103 degrees Fahrenheit. I was dehydrated and sick. I also fussed a great deal throughout the entire course of the day. Something was really wrong with me, and I was only three months old.

It would mark the first of many, many hospital visits I would make throughout my life.

The slow, steady beeping of the neonatal heart monitor showed the elevated heartbeats. There were a few IV tubes inserted into me, carrying the rehydrating properties of saline and water. The room was not brightly lit, as to prevent excessive light from going into my sensitive eyes. My cries showed protest and indignation at being invaded with sharp needles and strange people. Doctors and nurses came and went. They checked on me every few minutes.

Soon, everybody found out what happened. I had contracted spinal meningitis: a virus that could potentially rob you of your life, especially if you were a newborn.

Three people never left my side: Mommy, Father, and Grandmother.

I was looking at death in the eyes. It was my time to go, but I wasn't ready to give up. I was too selfish and stubborn. I wanted to stay. I wouldn't have been able to without the love of my family. Indeed, there is a story about how I came back to life.

During this period, one night, my grandmother held her hand over my forehead and prayed as much as she could. She knew I was dehydrated, that I could not produce tears. Mommy and Father couldn't handle it. They had to step outside for a while because they could not deal with the reality of the situation. It was hard on them. Grandmother could always be counted on. She prayed and recited many passages from the Bible. She bade me well as she left the room for the night. She also had a hard time. It wasn't easy for her, but she didn't want to cry in front of anybody. In addition, Grandfather Tom also came over and atoned me with oil and said prayers on the same evening that this happened.

The next day, something changed. My temperature dropped to normal levels, and my heartbeats were normal again. My heart was happy and strong. And I was crying, and there were real tears flowing down my face. I was no longer dehydrated, nor was I anywhere close to death. I had escaped, just as death was ready to snatch me away. God had intervened and blessed me with a second chance.

I survived.

But something else happened, something that nobody would really discover until one day later, when Mommy noticed there was something wrong with me.

Clang! The kitchen pot fell to the floor. Mommy was washing dishes and had dropped a pot. It was three months later, after my near-death experience. I was nearby in the living room in the crib. Acting on instinct, Mommy spun around and made sure the sound didn't wake me up. But I slept soundly. Puzzled, she continued doing the dishes.

Over a period of weeks, she didn't really think much of it until she noticed that I wasn't responding to sounds as a normal six-month-old child should. *Maybe it's just an ear infection again. He gets those so often.* One day, she decided to check my ears. They seemed fine, but she decided to do a test: she sat me down in the middle of the living room floor and slowly walked around behind me.

She clapped loudly. I remained on the floor, clueless, and did not react.

Again, another round of claps. I didn't respond. A cold sheet of panic rippled throughout her body. Rummaging through the closet, she extracted a vacuum cleaner. I watched Mommy from the living room, curious and expressionless. My head wobbled ever so slightly as I watched the tall figure drag a strange object.

Mommy had gone behind my back again. She unwound the cords and inserted the plug into the socket. And she clicked the vacuum on. The loud, droning sound of the vacuum cleaner filled the air like a million buzzing bees. Still, I did not respond. I was transfixed on some bright objects placed in front of me on the floor. Turning off the vacuum cleaner, Mommy placed a hand over her heart.

She slowly came up to me from behind. She tapped my shoulder. I reacted immediately, looking up to her, smiling. She put the hand over her mouth. Mommy now knew it was true.

Her son was Deaf.

"Diana, your son has profound hearing loss. He cannot hear anything below one hundred decibels. Maybe a little bit more in the right ear, but the left ear is no good. I'm so sorry. Would you like to talk about what we can do for him?" the audiologist asked Mommy after conducting a hearing test on me. The audiologist had a sad expression on her face.

Repressing the urge to cry, she held me on her lap and nodded. What was she going to do? What could she do to help me? She didn't know what to do. Cochlear implants? Hearing aids? Speech therapy? Sign language? Cued speech? Deaf school? Regular school? *How is all this going to work*, she wondered after learning all the options. It was 1980, and services for the Deaf and hard-of-hearing were still in its developmental stages.

The virus didn't claim my life, but it took away the gift of hearing. And it would affect me for the rest of my life.

Twenty-seven years later in 2006, I began to reflect on my own life. I had been doing that since I graduated from Gallaudet University, the world's only liberal arts university for the Deaf and hard-of-hearing, located in Washington, DC, when I was twenty-five. After graduation, I didn't really get a grasp on a career. I just didn't know what I wanted to do. Sure, people told me that I'm smart, but they also said I needed to settle down.

But there was so much unfinished emotional business within me. The silence within me was so loud that I had to listen to it. I began looking through photos: albums of the family, of the holidays. As I looked through them, I could make out an undeniable sequence of ups and downs in my life just by looking at the pictures.

The walk down memory lane was full of sadness and happiness. And photos are worth a thousand words in themselves.

———————————————————

Click. Christmas 1979. It was the first family gathering. I was barely a month old. In the picture, I see my mother on the left, with her perm, holding me. My father was on the right, with that long, hippie-style hair, holding me as well. They were the centerpiece with everybody on my mother's side surrounding them. I looked so tiny. Too young to have a personality or facial expressions. The glimmering threads of silver tinsels seemed to twinkle while being draped over the Christmas tree behind them.

Click. It was November 28, 1980. It was my first birthday. I see both my parents. I see balloons and a cute little cake. It would also be the last time I'd see a photo of my mother and my biological father surrounding me. I was sitting in a high chair, staring at the cake, with Mommy on the left and Father on the right. I had an expression of curiosity and awe.

Click. March 1984. I am holding my sister, who was

just born. I am beaming at the joy of having a sibling. I was so happy and fiercely protective of my new sister.

Click. January 1985. A formal portrait of me and Mommy. I sit there on her lap, smiling happily. I am wearing a Dallas Cowboys jersey, which was barely visible in the picture. Mommy is sitting there, with a model's body and a beautiful face. She had begun modeling in the early '80s. This is my favorite picture of me and Mommy. Her strong features and the beautiful, demure smile also show her strong, determined personality.

Click. It was Christmas 1986. I see a blond-haired, blue-eyed, happy child dressed in a pastel yellow sweater with a big bear on the front, those things that are puff-painted on. The same Christmas tree with its tinsels stood behind me. Most of my Christmases were spent at Grandmother's. This is one of my favorite pictures. I was such a happy child.

Click. March 1990. I am in a hospital room. I had sustained a serious injury while go-carting. The right eye is covered in a patch. Mommy is sitting next to me. This showed the beginning of the difficulties in my life: the physical accidents, the loss of perfect sight in my right eye due to a detached retina, the confusing years of preadolescence. I look insecure in the picture, almost as if I didn't want Mommy near me.

Click. Fall 1991. I see a school picture. I have gained weight, not obese, but I had eaten quite a bit that year. I look chubby. Years later, I would battle my weight from time to time.

Click. August 1994. I see a picture of my mother and me. We are in the mountains near Aspen, Colorado. Mommy is signing to me in American Sign Language, and I am holding a Styrofoam cup, listening to her with a smile on my face. This was when she took me to my first summer camp in the mountains in Colorado. I look happy in this picture. I was very excited to go away for a few weeks. I had started my growth spurts, thus causing me to return to a normal body weight.

Click. August 1995. It is my second year at camp, backpacking. I am in the Maroon Bells-Snowmass mountain chain. There is a trace of deep depression on my face. There are emotions that have begun to develop, confusion and conflict. This is a bittersweet picture for me, for I was sitting on the top of the peak of the most beautiful mountain in the West, yet I was so sad.

Click. May 1997. A graduation party in the backyard of my Grandmother's house. I finally had graduated, and my family gave me a nice little reception. I stood next to my future stepfather, Ken. I would later call him Dad. In this picture, I am wearing my red graduation gown from Westmoore High School. I was so happy, yet I looked a little scared and confused. Was I ready for college? I had gone through a lot during my senior year, what with my depression, therapy, and anger.

Click. August 1997. Orlando, Florida. Grandmother had recently relocated to Florida. We are at American Gladiators, one of their dinner theaters. My sister had come to visit. With her bleach-blond hair and fierce eyes, she poses like a gladiator. I am posing with a tanned face and a goofy smile, and my Grandmother is posing between us, with her smile that reminds me of the late Jacqueline Kennedy Onassis and the actress Susan Lucci. I had a fantastic summer and was ready for college.

Click. August 1997. In this photo I took a quick pose with my Mommy, right before I hopped onto the plane to Washington, DC for college. I was running late and didn't have much time to say good-bye. We look stressed out. It was really such a brief good-bye. I wish we would have spent more time together.

Click. November 1997. I had shaved my head, perhaps as a sign of rebellion, being away from home in the first time in years. I am surrounded with new friends in this photo. Life in Washington, DC was distracting and full of sinful temptations.

Click. December 1997. I visit New York City for the first time. I see myself in Central Park. It was a wonderful afternoon.

Click. May 12, 2005. I am on a dinner cruise on the ship, the *Odyssey*, in Washington, DC before graduation day. Aunt Julie and Grandmother were with me. In the picture, I am standing on the boat and Georgetown is behind me. And the Potomac River is beautiful. I look happy, but there are traces of a depressed, stressed-out young man.

Click. May 13, 2005. My graduation day at Gallaudet University. I see families from both sides of Mommy and Dad. It's a large group of people, and we all look happy, yet stressed out, stress that comes with a huge graduation event.

Click. February 2006. Melbourne, Florida. It is a joyful picture. My sister, Christina, had married and given birth to a beautiful girl named Julianna. She is holding the baby on the left. Mommy is on the right. Dad, Ryan, my brother-in-law, and I are surrounding Christina and Mommy. Julianna is barely a month old. It is a happy picture. I'm bleach-blonde and tanned to the core since I was enjoying the peace and quiet of Florida.

Click. February 2006. Same place. I am holding my

new niece, Julianna, and Mommy is next to me. I look happy, and a baby does look good in my arms. One day, I may want a child of my own.

Click. July 2007. A picture taken by my pager phone. I look quiet and peaceful. The medication has finally worked after years and years of searching for a right combination of medication. I look peaceful, yet I look tired and lonely. I had been away from home for more than a year.

More photos are there, but I had chosen a few that were the most memorable. The photographic journey reminded me of how much a person can evolve, change, and grow, and how many things that are thrown your way can be either a hindrance or a positive challenge.

I bring this up because I had a happy childhood. Mommy, Grandmother, and Aunt Julie, along with my sister, had learned how to sign, and I learned sign language first before trying out speech therapy. I had hearing aids. Mommy had decided against cochlear implants. She felt it was my decision to make, should I ever get to that point.

However, during my adolescent years, I developed a series of clinical problems: depression, anxiety, ADHD, and an addictive personality disorder. The hormones had aggravated these conditions, and it was not until well into my college years that I was finally able to assume control of those things. It was truly a torture trying to find the right combination of medication and cognitive and behavioral therapy.

I only bring this up because it is not a crime to be labeled "crazy." We all are crazy and quirky in our own ways. Indeed, my Aunt Julie always told me, "Everybody got their own quirks!" It's okay to have these problems. You are not defined by your weaknesses. You are defined by how you take control of those problems. That's what character is all about.

My closest friends and family have taught me that. And I'm forever in their debt.

To rise as a new soul above the old, tired one takes work. It is not a process that can be explained in the simplest terms. You have to experience it. The sweet, happy feeling of having finally shed your old self is priceless.

I only hope that this story will help many others who may find themselves in similar situations. Always know that the journey to self-actualization is always a very painful one, one that does not come to you automatically. You must make the choice to go through it. And you will come out at the other end a new person.

THE LIBRARIAN

Each one of us has some type of model for how our mind works. And when asked how to describe our minds, a lot of us run into a brick wall. I took a great deal in thinking about how to best present the world inside my mind.

The mind of a Deaf man is rich in visual symbolism and metaphors.

Here is how my mind works.

The master opened the grand, old steel door to a building. The dust escaped the room and penetrated the man's nostrils. The smell of acid paper and new paper also invaded his nose. He opened the door slowly, for he had not opened the door in a while. He had forgotten about himself and his love for life.

It was time to open the vault, to see and remember his dreams, to review what he had done so far with his life. He had recovered from a rough period; he was then ready to sit down and look through the intricate web that he called his own life.

The afternoon sunlight flowed through the massive, round, stain-glassed window and bathed the ancient library in a soft, colorful, luminous light. The light fell upon stacks and stacks of old, dusty textbooks, textbooks from an earlier period of his life, books he had ever so diligently collected over the course of his lifetime. Thousands and thousands of classics, some in foreign languages, lie there.

The Deaf man has always loved languages, languages and cultures from far-off places, places he had always dreamed of going to, places far away from his little suburban town of Moore, Oklahoma. He may not hear the exact utterances of those languages when spoken, but he could always count on the written records of languages. Proof. Consistency. Credibility. Those were the major elements acting as advantages to the written medium.

He didn't listen to those who said he lacked the ability to acquire a second language because of his hearing impairment. Indeed, the master turned his nose up at those who said that and proceeded to learn, not a second or third, but a fourth language. He is proud of his achievements, yet he is humble. He is afraid to talk about his achievements. He learned very quickly that there lurked many people in corners that might reject you because of your achievements. He could not afford to lose his new friends, friends he didn't have when he was growing up. He was afraid. Friends were so important to him.

The high, domed ceiling, with its mural of the greatest artists of the Renaissance period, provided a safe umbrella above this ancient library. The great classical marble columns ensured that the structure would never collapse, even under the greatest stress or duress. The library is eleven stories high, built in a completely circular structure, and access to each door on each floor is restricted.

Each door requires a very special key, a key that only the master carried.

The master did not trust anybody else to see or read his thoughts, goals, dreams, or the innermost feelings. For the longest time, the master did not reveal himself too much to others. He didn't care if they called him arrogant, cold, self-centered, or just simply weird. The master was just simply trying to protect himself. He was too sensitive to the outside world. He couldn't handle the world, the world that seemed to laugh at and mock him.

He was safe inside his library, where the books would never laugh at him, where the books opened themselves and welcomed the tired, stressed-out, young Deaf man into their worlds. He always welcomed their adventures, journeys, and new inspirations. The master understood books and written papers. He understood order and structure. It was the only place the master felt he could be truly himself. It was his escape, an escape from reality.

Everything inside the ancient library had been painstakingly catalogued by the master. A great deal of time was put into the organization of the master's life. There are ten doors inside the library, one on each level, except on the first. They are categorized in order of importance. What the master feels comfortable with others seeing lies on the old, dusty marble floor. The deep blue, Venetian marble gleams underneath the stacks of books. Those books are fine for public viewing, but the doors above the main floor are securely locked, some that had not been opened in decades.

The master had worked very hard to keep those doors of yesterday away from the public eye. He did not want the world to see how fragile he was. Nor did he want anybody to identify his weaknesses and use them against him. However, the master knew that it was now time to look inside those doors and come to peace with the things inside. Only then would he be happier and more secure with himself and his place in the world outside the ancient library.

Soaking in the warm afternoon sunlight and looking at the soft colors dancing on the marble floor, the master looks up to the great, domed ceiling of the library and smiles.

He was now home.

This is the library of my mind and soul, and I am the librarian.

A library represents an extraordinary wealth of information and knowledge; it also represents peace and serenity, in addition to order and function. In physical terms, a library is always a place where one could go and contemplate about life or at least lose oneself in the books provided by the library. I remember the first time I went to a library and actually experienced it. It was the public library in Moore, Oklahoma. I was only ten years old. This tiny library seemed to have all the books of my heart's desire. It was amazing to me how a tiny library could have packed all those books into a small, singular space.

That began my love for the written language, a medium that had proven itself to me over the years; it was stable, consistent, controlled, and well thought-out. I didn't have to worry about deciphering the spoken language through lip reading or even sign language because it was just "too much work" for me. I was experiencing the early stages of ADHD, and it didn't help that I was still working on speech therapy. There was simply too much room for misunderstandings and mistakes. Perhaps that's why I was such a bookworm, a nerd if you will, in school.

Over the years, as I got older and life seemed to become more stressful, the ancient library became my own secret garden. When I was a child, I had many dreams. And they drifted farther and farther away from me as I became depressed because I had realized it was difficult to even begin the path toward those dreams. One by one, my dreams were tossed aside into my secret garden until many years later, I'd find them again. Some dreams would remain dreams, but there are others that the little boy in me still wants to achieve.

The master pulled out an old, oak ladder from the small utility closet on the mezzanine floor. He looked up to the floors of the circular library. He needed to look inside the rooms. Pondering this question, he ignited one of the glass globes that had oil in it and pulled it off the wall. He then proceeded to move the ladder to the trapdoor leading to the second floor because it was time for him to look at the first door named "Dreams Lost."

After having climbed the shaky, old ladder, he reached the second floor. He got on and walked toward the door. With a rusty hand, he fiddled through his bag and found the antique golden key. The evening had passed. It was now pitch-black dark outside, and the only source of light was pulsating from the glass globe in his hand. He pressed the head of the key into the hole of the doorknob. It clicked, and the master pushed the door open. The creaking of the door sounded like someone scratching the chalkboard; the master shivered at the sensation.

He entered the dusty, old room. Inside, there were various childhood toys: a wooden pony, a painting set, some puzzles, those typical things you would find for a young boy. The glass globe's light illuminated the room. The windows in the room were covered with a heavy, black velvet drape. Directly in front of him there stood a life-sized portrait of his younger self, a happy, quixotic child sitting on a maroon-colored Davenport seat dressed in his school clothes, his back straight and proud, with a German shepherd at his foot. Carrying a curious, peaceful expression, the blond-haired boy stared back at him.

The portrait of Joshua showed a child full of dreams and happiness. The master stared at the portrait for the longest time. How extraordinary! How so much he had forgotten how he looked back then! The portrait looked nothing like him. He was no longer that child. Life's disappointments and pains had drawn themselves on the master's face.

He then looked around the room. He saw some notebook papers on a desk. He approached them and examined the papers. The master recognized them immediately. They were dreams of a little boy, dreams that were given to him by his mother and family members. His mother told him he could do anything he wanted to do. They were goals written on separate sheets of notebook paper, written in that messy handwriting that comes with being young and left-handed. The papers showed the dreams of the younger Joshua.

I want to be an actor. This was written and there were many stars surrounding it, some in glitter that had fallen on stars shaped by glue. Today, the dream is still very much alive.

I want to be a model. Dozens and dozens of pictures from the children's catalog from Sears and JCPenney's adorned this piece of paper. It would be nice to do some modeling. But it's not a priority now.

I want to be a lawyer. The picture of the blindfolded Lady Justice balancing the scales was drawn below the sentence. This dream will never go away. The master still has law school on his sights. He wants to help many, many people.

I want to be a writer. This was written with images of book after book. And a happy face was drawn, in addition to a huge exclamation mark. This dream has almost come true for the young Joshua. This is the first piece of work, and the master is determined to spread the story in the best way possible; this is not about personal gain. This is about helping others through the gift of storytelling. Here is a story of overcoming challenges and finding the beauty and peace within oneself.

I want to be a Nobel Prize-winning scientist. This was written with "Marie Curie, the girl that won the Nobel Prize. I wanna discover a new element just like her."

I want to be an astronaut. Various images of the Space Shuttle *Challenger* before its demise were plastered on this one. The master really wanted to do this. But people with disabilities have a very hard time getting into any space programs. And the high risk involved in traveling to outer space had prompted him to think twice.

The master sighed and knew that those dreams were the ones he had made a long time ago. For the longest time, he stared at his younger self in the portrait. The boy looked back at him, his happy expression perpetually frozen in time.

Why can't I be happy like that all the time? I wish I could stay that happy, he thought to himself.

He then released a great, sad sigh and turned around. He walked toward the door and left the room, shut the door, and locked it. While closing the door, he subconsciously wiped away the cobwebs that had formed around the door. He polished the brass plaque with that "my dreams" title. He stood there with a blank expression, staring at the plaque.

My Dreams. My Dreams. My Dreams. The words kept playing over and over in his head. The master no longer knew what his dreams were or are. He felt so lost. Vacant. Meaningless. Insignificant. He took a long, steadying breath and re–centered himself. The master pressed his forehead upon the cold, brass plaque and closed his eyes.

I don't understand how I could have forgotten my dreams, the master thought with a heavy heart. A shudder, the one that always comes before a violent sob, ran through his body as he pictured the young boy in the portrait. He dropped to the floor and had a good cry.

I stopped believing in myself a long time ago. How exactly it happened, I'm not certain. But somewhere down the road, the discrimination and the sneers from the outside world had become too much for me. It was just too much. I began to settle for second best. I looked for the easiest routes in life and education. I just couldn't handle it, the additional stresses.

I'll admit it: it was hard for me to grow up. I always

wanted to stay a child. I still do from time to time, not because I was immature or irresponsible. It was just that I didn't have the strength to face the world and the obstacles. And I missed the happiness from that period of my life. I really did. I did everything I could to keep some of that happiness. But it seemed to slip through my stubborn fingers, fingers that seemed not to understand the rules of the game. So many times, I wanted to stay home with Mommy and Dad for the longest time possible. The boy in the corner didn't want to leave the security of his home.

The master was now on the third floor. The second door was labeled "One Who Never Left Me." He smiled at the thought of this room and almost eagerly unlocked the door and went inside.

The portrait in this room also showed a slightly older Joshua, perhaps in third or fourth grade, sitting next to a beautiful woman whom the master knew as his mother. In the room, he saw many objects: sign language books, hearing aids and batteries, addresses and telephone numbers of specialists, and some classroom pictures. The room was full of things you'd expect to see for a serious young student. It was also full of other things. His mother had studied every option possible for him; she made the difficult choices, hoping that one day they would prove to be good ones. She also never abandoned the young Joshua, no matter how difficult the circumstances became. She was always there for him.

In the room there are also presents and birthday cakes everywhere. There are also plates and plates full of fresh food, food that had just been baked and fried. Every time the master goes in this room, for some reason, there was always food. And they were freshly made. It was almost as if the mother in the portrait of Joshua secretly crept out of the frame, placed some food on the tables, making sure her son in real life would be well-fed, upon hearing the master's distant, approaching footsteps.

The master's mother had always ensured that her son was well provided for. She always showered him with gifts and love, in addition to her excellent regional cooking, discipline, and her wisdom. She was his hero, an unacknowledged hero, who had always inspired him. She had given so much to raising him. There were times when he didn't treat her with respect. He had treated her terribly a few times over his lifetime.

But she always forgave me. Even though when I was going through my anger years, when I successfully pushed everybody away because I felt so horrible about myself, she stood by me. Granted, she threw her hands up in the air a lot. But the point here is she loved me. She still does. You can't ask for anything better than the love of your own mother.

Exiting the room, the master took one final whiff of the aroma of deep fried chicken and smiled. He also looked at his mother in the portrait. The mother seemed to smile back, and the master thought he saw a quick wink. He was happy. He locked the door and sat down on the floor, lost in thought.

My mother is the best person in the world. That's how I would put it. Our relationship had become intricately tied, a relationship that is forged through years of love in spite of difficult times. I love her so much. I cannot imagine my life without her. She doesn't know it, but many times, she had saved me from myself. She was there for me and was my best friend during the times when I didn't have any friends at all.

Holding up the handle to the blazing glass globe, the master leaned over the railing and looked up to the railings of the fourth and fifth floors. He knew what doors were there. Releasing a trapdoor that led him to the fourth floor, he placed the ladder and climbed it. "Interruptions," the plaque read on the third door. Those years were his formative years. The master knew the room would be overflowing with objects. Clicking the shiny, golden antique key into the hole, he found it hard to open the door. The room was just so full.

Bracing himself for an inevitable tsunami of possessions, he closed his eyes and pushed the door forward as hard as he could.

The objects flowed out of the room with a surprisingly easy, one-time stroke of motion. It knocked the master over. He got up and looked inside the room. There were several portraits of his younger self, all lined up in the back against the covered windows. Some of them were covered with a thin, white sheet, as if someone hastily covered it, ashamed to see it.

The master uncovered the portraits. What he saw caught him off-guard. Some of the portraits bore the ugly characteristics that you would find in a soul that had sinned quite often. Some of them carried an expression of sadness and frustration. Rejection, anger, depression, and angst were written all over the faces of some of the portraits.

The negative emotions ruined an otherwise nice face on many of the portraits. They stood out among the different portraits where there wasn't any negativity. The different stages of his life were evident in those portraits.

He then left the room. It was a room he would just have to come back to later. It was not exactly his favorite room, but it was crucial that he examine his past, a past full of lessons. His life was never easy. He learned many things the hard way, and he would rather forget about them. But one must love oneself and understand oneself before being capable of love and success in every possible way. And that meant learning from his past.

With a sigh of disgust, the master locked the door.

He was now on the fifth floor. He stared at the door in front of him. The plaque read, "The Stabilizer."

"Hey, Josh. Listen to me carefully. I love this guy very much, and please don't scare him or drive him away. I need someone in my life, okay? I really love him," my mother said to me one day. I was in her bedroom, and she was putting on perfume and checking her hair. She was also checking her dress in front of the full-length mirror. She had an anxious look on her face.

It was 1997. I was a senior in high school, and Mommy was dating someone. She was getting ready for a first, formal date. The date, Ken, was coming over to the house shortly. I didn't like the idea since every guy she went out with seemed to hurt her. I was protective of her. She had gone through a couple divorces. And the Oedipus complex in me was an annoying one. I always found a way to freak out whomever Mommy would be dating. I did my best to push them out. They were not welcome. I didn't want them to come in and assume authority that wasn't Mommy's.

"Okay. I promise," I said after seeing a slight hint of desperation in Mommy's eyes. I could tell she loved this man very much.

Well, at least she would have someone while I'm gone in college. It won't last long, but at least she'd have someone, I thought to myself.

Boy, was I wrong.

"Oh thank you, Josh. Can you please make sure he is comfortable when he gets here? Please don't forget your manners. Offer him water or something and let him know I'll be running a little bit late," Mommy said.

"Okay, Mom," I said with a smile.

"By the way, Josh, how do I look?" she inquired with a nervous, excited smile.

"Mom, you always look great," I replied with an exasperated sigh. She gave me a humorous, dismissive wave of the hand and went into the bathroom of the master bedroom. And I headed out to the living room and waited for this new visitor.

Mommy and I have this little thing. Anytime we would go out, we always ask each other this very fundamental question: How do I look? It's one of those little things we always had. We still do that even to this day. A few minutes later, the doorbell rang. My hearing aid detected the sound, and I walked to the front door. I opened it and looked at the figure in front of me. The man was dressed sharply, and he was sporting a military haircut. He was in the Air Force, according to Mommy. He was holding some flowers. He greeted me with a strong, yet respectful and sensitive voice.

"Hello, Joshua. My name is Ken." He extended his hand. I shook his hand while giving him the usual critical look that I always gave to new strangers. But I could see in his eyes that he was trying to make a connection with me. I just didn't want to see it at that time.

"Hi, Ken. Please, won't you come in?" I said with a polite smile. I could tell Mommy really liked this person. And that was how I met my future stepfather, whom I call Dad now. He would be the best thing that happened to the family.

The master didn't even have to go into this door. He already knew that this room was a simple one, a room formed during his later years. He knew the room was clean and organized, for his new Dad was a clean-cut introduction into his life, an introduction that stabilized the family and gave it order and efficiency, in addition to unparalleled love. Dad was also an incredibly sensitive man with good, old-fashioned family values. There's just something about him that cannot be described in words. His silent resolve in the face of adversity has inspired the master for the last ten years. The master didn't need to look at the portrait either. He knew the portrait would be one of pride and happiness. Joshua now had a complete family unit.

However, when he got to the sixth floor in search for the fifth door, the master gasped. A huge mirror was standing next to the door. He could see his reflection. He had forgotten about this sinister mirror. This room has haunted him all his life. It was a hard room to look into, for one is forced to look at oneself in the mirror. Indeed, the room was called "The Room of Mirrors." In this room there were no portraits. No prefabri-cated objects. It's just full of mirrors, and this room forced a person to look at himself as he was. And the most used mirror in this room was the bath-room mirror. The master has looked at himself everyday in the bathroom while preparing himself for the world. This mirror does not lie. It does not deceive. You are as you are in front of this mirror, as it is always located in the most private room of any residence; here, a person lets himself go, drops all pretenses, and that is when the moment of unseen ugliness or beauty reveals itself.

The bathroom mirror was also a place where visual reflections of goals, dreams, and feelings came alive. The person on the other side of the mirror became very real, and the master could never escape that person. The person becomes the conscience of the viewer, an inevitable monitor of his soul. A veritable gold mine of insight, the mir-ror is to be used wisely. He dared not enter this room, at least not just yet. The master didn't want to have to deal with his own reflection. He just wanted to do a run-through of what was in his life. He'll come back soon.

Dragging the old ladder, he saw there were more doors. Time had passed quickly. The early dawn light was slowly illuminating the dark sky. Yet, the task self-presented by the master must be accomplished. The master pressed on.

Upon arriving to the seventh floor, he walked to the sixth door labeled, "Sweet November." The master smiled because this is one of his favorite rooms, in addition to the fact that the month of November always brought to him the best things, for some reason. He opened the door after unlock-ing it. The bright, shimmering hues of beauty radiated from the room like an ethereal, heavenly light.

Everything in this room made sense to the master, for everything in this room represented beauty. In this room, every type of beauty could be found. The master had always loved beautiful things, for they helped ease his emotional pain of being Deaf. He knew his other senses were very valuable, and he wanted to enjoy life as much as possible. Even the usual portrait was different. He becomes emotional in this room, for when he is surrounded by some exquisitely beautiful things, he cannot help but feel that everything wouldn't be so bad after all, like a child getting some candy.

The portrait showed Joshua as the man inside the painting *The Geographer* by the Dutch painter, Johannes Vermeer. Always an explorer at heart, the master saw himself in the painting. The master had always felt that his mind also represented the nuances of a beautiful Vermeer masterpiece, in terms of the colorful imagination and the kaleidoscope of languages. The fine arts had always been a huge part of the master's life. Years and years were spent cultivating an in-depth knowledge of the art world, especially anything from the French culture. He had even pursued a bachelor's in French at Gallaudet University. That was how much he loved art and languages, particularly the language of French. In the opinion of the master, the French did not only understand art, they lived it. They breathed it. It became their very existence. And the master duplicated that, integrating it into the file cabinets of the library.

Indeed, one could find, in a corner of the room, a small group of paintings by Monet, Renoir, Manet, and the master's personal favorite,

Degas. These paintings were what he had liked in museums. They were copies, as one couldn't certainly afford the originals. The incredible strokes of diffused color and light used in the cutting-edge period of French Impressionism made those paintings special to the master.

They weren't perfect paintings by artistic standards of that period, but something about it made sense. It was real, but it also became a dream, a dream within a reality. The painter Degas always made the master think of ballet. Ballet, with its sweet, soft, controlled movements in sync to the carefully orchestrated and choreographed music, brought the master to a very happy, childlike place. Also, in that corner, there were some compact discs of the greatest opera singers in the world, including Maria Callas and Charlotte Church. There were also countless programs of plays, theatres, and operas stacked on the floor from earlier days.

Hearing aids had helped the master obtain a sample of what music had to offer. He had always particularly loved the world of opera, for his hearing aids always picked up the extraordinarily beautiful high voices of the soprano singers. He may be Deaf, but as long as the master had his hearing aids, he could hear the highest notes of the entire opera, usually those from the female singers, for their pitch was so strong and beautiful. Something about it moved mountains and valleys for the master. Something about it inspired him to visualize nothing but great, big things that he would want to do for himself in the future.

He didn't care about the fact that he couldn't understand the lyrics, even if they were in English. What was more important was that the master could actually hear something, and he could take what he heard and create his own opera inside his library, where the only audience was himself. The sound of music was very much alive within the master.

The master also loved antiques. He could not get enough of those priceless objects. He loved the way they sparkled and how they sent him a message from the days of yesterday, a message that was subtly hidden in the wear and tear of the object. You had to be appreciative to understand it.

In another corner there sat a dozen lamps from Tiffany & Co., which were ever so brilliantly designed by Louis Comfort Tiffany. There were antiques everywhere in that particular corner, most of them precious stones, ancient velvet tapestries, and more unclassified antiques that were too interesting to throw away. There were other objects of beauty in the room, more than one could count. However, there were a couple of books. These books were not antiques. But they were the tragically beautiful stories that the master had come across that still tugged at his heart. There were two children books: *Pinocchio* and *The Velveteen Rabbit*. These books were for children, yes. But their very simplicity also made the books endearing to adults too. Each one of these stories ended with a "comeback" or an "emergence of a new person." Each was a product of a metamorphosis.

At Red Oak Elementary School, in my classroom, I saw a book on the desk of the teacher. It seemed to be a new one. I asked if I could look at it. The teacher gave it to me with a smile. I was in second grade, and I remember that day being cold, since it was late November of 1987. On the cover there was a colorful picture of a wooden puppet with a long nose. The book was called *Pinocchio*. I was as little bit behind in learning all the typical stuff because I was compensating for my hearing loss. It is a lot of work trying to make up for it in terms of language acquisition and education.

I first learned about a boy that was not real, but he became real later on. He was this wooden puppet made by the woodcarver; he was lonely and wanted a son. At first, Pinocchio didn't realize there was anything wrong with him. Over time, he began to realize he wasn't like the other boys. Geppetto didn't care. He loved him very much and encouraged him to be a normal boy as much as possible. Pinocchio wanted to change. He wanted to be just like the other boys. After a crazy period where he became lost and almost broke Geppetto's heart, he came back home. And he wanted his "father" back. Geppetto had gone out to search for him. And that night, when he wished upon the star so the woodcarver could come back, the Blue Fairy came. She told Pinocchio that since he had an unselfish heart, he deserved the greatest reward: to be a normal human boy. She then tapped him with her wand. The light blue light surrounded the puppet. And he became real. He was now normal in every way. And the story ended as everybody knows it.

I know I am not a wooden puppet. I am so far from that. But I was in second grade, and I was ready to take on problems and challenges. Indeed, that was when I really realized I was different than the other boys. Something was wrong with me. I knew I wasn't made out of wood, naturally, but I felt I needed to get my ears fixed.

After reading the book, I really began to feel bad about being different. I was put into the early Deaf education program, where they typically put Deaf children at the beginning to adjust them to the public school system. I noticed quickly that I was separated from other hearing students and wondered why. I started to understand when I had a hard time talking to others verbally. Mind you, this was in second grade, and I was just starting on basic speech therapy. I still had a lot of ground to cover. But I realized I was really Deaf when I couldn't speak well. I was getting frustrated. Because of this, I was determined to be as normal as possible, to fit in, and then maybe I'd have more friends and be happier. Indeed, I decided to do something about it.

Mommy never knew this, but for three straight weeks in December of 1987, I wrote to the Blue Fairy, asking her what star I should wish upon and when she would please come see me. Every night for three weeks, I wrote a letter, in an awkward early writing style, to the Blue Fairy. And it was something like this, give or take:

> Dear Blue Fairy,
>
> My name is Josh. I read about you in the book. You are so pretty and nice. I know you can help me. What star do I wish on? Please. My ears are made of wood. I cannot hear. Can you please make them real again? Help me hear. I can't speak very well. Please help me.
>
> Sincerely yours,
> Josh

I worked so hard on that note. And I would rewrite one every single night because I kept thinking she wouldn't come because I had made a spelling error. I thought I did something to upset her. I would look outside every night and search the cold, starry night sky for that blue ball of color or at least something that would be moving toward my bedroom window. I needed her and was very anxious to see her. I had also seen the Walt Disney movie version, and I truly believed that she would float into my bedroom and fill it with light and that she'd tell me how good I had been, and I would tell her that I was helping Mommy more around the house with the chores. And then she would make everything okay again. I even wanted to ask the Blue Fairy to make my mother happy because she seemed so sad sometimes. I was planning on asking the fairy to tap her with her wand and make her not worry about anything.

I'm not sure what I wrote word-for-word, but I do remember this: each day when I realized I still was not able to hear, I was upset. I tried to rationalize it. I tried to, with my limited writing skills, look at the mistakes. I didn't want to let Mommy know. I wanted to surprise her when I could hear again. Then Mommy wouldn't have to worry about special arrangements for school. At that age, I remember seeing my mother looking sad when she was looking at me every once in a while. She occasionally would join me in the kitchen, and she would ask me to tell her stories and tell her what I did for the day. She seemed to want to hear about what was going on with me.

I didn't know what was going on, but I could read her face and tell she was sad about something. And this went on for three weeks. Each day passed, and with each day, a note was unread, still folded up neatly and tucked away inside a small envelope under my pillow. And a new note was written each night. I used up my allowance money and I sought the apartment for change so I could buy more paper so I could try to get a perfect note for such a busy fairy. And one day, I just gave up. After talking to the other Deaf students in my classroom, I learned that it was just a story, but it fed my heart with such hope. I felt like an idiot. I felt so stupid. It was something I really believed in. I believed that there were people out there that could come down and fix everything for you if you minded your manners and brushed your teeth every night before you went to bed.

If a wooden boy could get a real body and a real nose, then perhaps they could fix a simple thing like a broken set of ears. As I type this, I am reliving this experience. It's funny. It's been over twenty years, and this still affects me.

The next book was something I read much later in my life, probably when I was seventeen. It is strange, but this story went to my heart like a painful stab. The name of this wonderful children's book is *The Velveteen Rabbit*. This story moves me because it talks about a ragged toy rabbit that nobody wanted and how the other rabbits would make fun of him when he came alive; his skin wasn't as clean as theirs. His buttons were missing. He wasn't popular. He was just a toy bunny, not like the real ones out there in the garden. And because he thought he wasn't important, the velveteen rabbit pretty much gave up on life and allowed himself to be discarded into the trashcan.

The boy finds him, and he is so happy to see the rabbit. And the boy picks it up and tells the rabbit how much he loves him and how worried he was about him. The rabbit should have not listened to the other rabbits that said he was not important. He now knew that he was loved in spite of his shortcomings. He felt the love from the little boy, and he became alive the next morning.

He was now a real rabbit, a healthy happy rabbit. Love helped him flourish, and that love came from the most unexpected place. And because of love the velveteen rabbit finally got to be what he wanted to be: a real, live rabbit who could eat on greens with the other rabbits in the garden. The velveteen rabbit was finally accepted by his peers. If only it was that simple for many of us.

I am sure some of you know only too well the feeling of not being completely accepted. Sure, people will be polite to you, but you're never really a part of the group. You try. You work hard. You go out of your way. And still, people just don't seem to want to work harder to get to know you, especially if you had a lot to offer as a friend. *The Velveteen Rabbit* is the epitome of how one person, no matter who, could make all the difference in the world to someone. All it takes is one person to love another, and the person who gets that love is the luckiest person in the world. That's how it should be.

I hope to spread my story and experiences through doing what I do the best: writing. With writing, I hope I can reach at least one person during my lifetime with my story. And if I change that person's life for the better, then I am successful. With my sincerity and my radiating happiness, I hope I can reach the heart of one reader.

Just one.

The master put the children's books down back where he had retrieved them. It was time to leave the room. The radiant, ethereal glow from the room faded out as the master closed and locked the door. At the same time, the glass globe ran out of oil. And the flame inside dwindled. Fortunately, it was already morning. And another source of light was waiting for the master somewhere. And that somewhere was the next door. That room was called "God and Me."

He made his way to door number seven on level eight. Outside on the level, it was not bright, but it was not dark; it was early morning. Because of this and the fact that the glass globe had no oil, the master was not prepared for what happened next. He opened door seven after unlocking it. And immediately, he raised both of his arms to cover his eyes. He let out a shriek and fell backward and hit the floor.

The light burst out with such massive power, power like a hundred thousand chariots with horses running down from the heavens above; it blazed and reverberated throughout the entire library and rushed out of every available window. It bathed the library with a bright, white-hot light that shimmered like a moving ocean of tiny diamonds. And there was a beautiful, celestial choir full of operatic singing in the background that signaled the arrival of the messengers of the Lord.

Then something happened to the time. The huge grandfather clock's pendulum on the mezzanine floor froze. The master's watch and its hands froze. Time had been suspended. Time had stepped aside and gave way to the arriving party. Then the mood of the library changed. The air became alive again, only this time, time and space were taken out of the equation. The noise was gone, yet the quietness of the library became even more profound. And there was nothing but the wonderful feeling of relaxation and peace. And peace was there, which the master had always craved but had a hard time maintaining in his life. Everything moved so slowly and gracefully, almost as if the figures from the heavens above glided down to the earth. God was nowhere to be seen, but his messengers were there.

In place of the light, the darkness fled. The sadness and pain in the library and portraits disappeared. The anger faded away, too.

Out of the blue, he could see the angels and the master knew it was God greeting him.

Snapping out of his thoughts, the master scrambled to the closet inside the room, as this had happened before. He looked for the usual pair of sunglasses and put them on. With a satisfied sigh, he got to his feet and smiled. He was so transfixed by the scene happening before him, that he forgot all about his eyesight.

"Our Heavenly Father, which art in heaven, hallowed be thy name. Thank you for coming today. I needed it. Amen." The master recited his feelings into a short prayer. And he quickly added another sentence, almost wittingly. "Oh, by the way, feel free to stay around. I'll leave that door open. I love the feeling in this building right now. It's fantastic. I feel great. Please, won't you stay for a while?"

The master paused and decided he had done enough for the day. He would get to the final doors later. He wanted to enjoy the presence of the Lord and take a break from his life. He took these visits and conversations with God very seriously.

The master felt no pain or sorrow. He now has peace. And he is now the happy, radiant boy in the portrait, surrounded by this bright light. He is not shy or self-conscious. He is simply transported to the carefree days of yesteryear, the days in his childhood. As long as the light stays with him, his body and spirit is suspended in a state of perfection and serenity. That's how the master knows God is a very real presence, because the light explodes and overwhelms him each time he speaks with the Lord. And he feels the shimmering, rippling sheet of peace pass over him after he finishes a prayer. Just like that.

I have believed in God since day one, pretty much since I learned how to read and understand the concept of good and bad. My relationship with God is an honest and simple one, one that does not bear any pretenses. The relationship is a full one, too. It has humor, love, anger, and spiritual guidance. These are the elements within the relationship between God and me. There is one more element that I feel is worth mentioning.

When conversing with the Lord, I can completely let myself go, emotionally, and not be judged negatively for it. Only He knows what I have been through. He knows me more than I know myself. So I put my faith into something that transcends the law of physics and physical science. That is how much I believe in Him. What I feel is very real, and it all comes from the spiritual sphere of the light.

When I visited France for a brief time, there was a very significant quote—and it is used by the Catholic University of America in Washington, DC—that was carved into the entrance wall to one of those smaller, older Gothic churches in Paris. It was in Latin. And the inscription read *"Deus lux mea est."* The translation is *God is my light.*

It's the kind of light that violates the laws of known science. The kind of power that accounts for that occur on a daily basis on this planet. The kind of unseen power that can alter the course of your spiritual journey and help you undergo a metamorphosis; at the end, you emerge as a newborn, ready to take on the world all over again.

And always know you can find that light within yourself, too. You just have to know where to find it.

All people have their own way of classifying their minds and souls, ways of exploring the fundamental question of their purpose of being on the face of the earth.

The library requires a lot of work, and I'm proud to be the librarian of my mind and soul. I take great joy in keeping the library organized, as that helps me remain sane and content as I continue the never-ending quest for knowledge and priceless wisdom.

AN UNEXPECTED METAMORPHOSIS

I began to feel the immediate, defensive reaction quickly overtake my body; this happened each time someone would offer me advice or feedback. Forcing that reaction to take a backseat, I sat there, crossing my legs and putting my arms into the standard defensive position. I quickly assumed the well-known defensive body. I always could tell when Mommy wanted to talk to me about something I was doing. Twenty-seven years old, and I still acted like a child.

I was Deaf. They don't understand even half of the things I put up with. My life has been a struggle, and it's hard enough without people telling me what they think is best for me, I would always think when I'm asked why I'm so defensive.

Mommy and I were sitting outside in the sunroom at the house we were living in before she and Dad bought a new home. We were in Florida. I was on break from college. She was drinking her sweet iced tea, and a Diet Coke sat next to me on the side table. I took it and drank. The whirring fan cooled us down. It was another hot summer day in Florida. I had just vented to her a story about a conflict that had happened up at college a conflict with a friend. I could see Mommy was about to let out a deep sigh and tell me something. Over the years, I've learned which and what type of response would come out of my mother because of the closeness of our relationship. I could tell something was coming, something that would have to do with a small lecture.

> Inside the library, red flags started popping up. An emergency siren went off. The entire structure tensed up, and the contents on the marble floor panicked by jumping up and down, as if they were looking for a hiding place.
> But the librarian walked into the library and announced that it was not an attack. He then told the library and its contents to calm down and relax. He repeated it in a louder voice. The response was absolute silence.

The panic reflex gone, I exhaled. As she started to talk, I forced myself to listen and not open my mouth, as was the habit.

"Josh, listen to me," she started. I let out a silent scoff and rolled my eyes. *Why are you attacking me, Mommy? I didn't do anything to you.* My first reaction flew into my head.

"Oh, Mom." I let out a high-pitched whine.

Mommy took a more assertive position in her seat and raised her voice just ever so slightly. She then proceeded in both sign language and voicing.

"No, I'm serious. Josh, please stop it. I want to say something. You know I love you very, very much. I want nothing but the best for you. But you better listen, buddy. This stuff is getting too old. I can't do this every time," she said.

Sliding into my childlike state of mind, I started looking for a distraction. I darted my eyes to something in the background. I fidgeted in my seat. I felt my legs wanting to move up and down. I was distracted. And I didn't want to go through the process again. I just wanted to talk about my problem and leave it at that. I didn't want advice, nor did I want an opinion coming from my own mother. I just wanted to talk to someone quickly so I'd feel better. Her face followed me, so that I would look at her.

"Hey? I'm over here. Look at me. Listen to me, please."

I could see Mommy becoming impatient. She hated it when I looked away, especially when I didn't have my hearing aid on. My mind switched to a different thought very quickly. That thought was related to something she had told me earlier, something I've taken into account but forgot before I opened my mouth, which happened often.

When you talk about a problem, you have to be prepared for a reaction. Reactions are normal, and you better be prepared for an opinion, suggestion, advice, or whatever. You honestly cannot sit down, tell someone a big problem, then say, "Thanks, have a great day!" and scamper off. It's just not going to work. Each time you talk to a person, you are bringing him or her into the situation. Not into it, exactly, but you are presenting to him or her a problem that usually has nothing to do with him/her, and sometimes the person feels compelled to give something back, be it positive or negative. Think carefully before you share it. Use the concept and rules of necessity: Is it really necessary?

My mind flipped back to the channel where Mommy was sitting across from me and about to continue her lecture. I was shifting and not listening. I knew what that opening line usually meant. We had this type of conversation for years. It was getting old for both of us. There has to be another way of solving problems. While I snapped back into focus and took a sip of my Diet Coke, I listened to her. I also took a very long breath through my nostrils, as to calm myself down. I had to start accepting the fact that not everything is always going to be lovey-dovey between Mommy and me. That's life, the essence of real world. And sometimes you hear things you don't want to hear. And it might actually be good for you.

"You need to work on how to handle stress and problems. You haven't had much experience with the outside world. You have been in school all your life, and you've found a nice, safe place there. One of these days, you have to finish school. When you get older, you'll have stuff thrown in your face like you wouldn't believe. You have to really sit down and think about how to deal with it. You're good at thinking, Josh, but you just don't act on your plans. You come up with ideas, dreams, and plans, but you don't follow through with them. Start acting on your thoughts and solutions that you propose to yourself everyday. And keep your stress to a minimum. Don't add more stress to your life. And you may want to be nicer to people and not be so reactive. That's why you're having this problem in college right now. People don't know what the hell to expect from you. Sometimes you can be this, then the next day, that," the frustrated mother finished.

I sat there, and I was beginning to fall into one of my deep thoughts about how people perceived me. She continued.

"When you have a problem, you isolate it and then

you ask yourself a few questions: A) after determining that you have a problem on hand, can you solve it immediately? B) If yes, great. If not, can you solve it within the near future? C) If so, great. If not, can you cope with it?" She finished with an exasperated tone of voice. I nodded, but my face remained blank. I was absorbing the information. A concerned expression worked its way across her face, and she asked me a question that I hated the most.

"Are you taking your medication, Josh?" she asked gently.

"Yes! Yes, I been takin' it. Yes. Yes," I said with an extremely affronted tone of voice. My mouth tensed and my eyes became wide and my face became unpleasant. I had been taking my medication. And I know it helps.

Looking back, that question was not designed to attack me in any way. It was just an honest question, a question that every family member or friend would ask. When someone is concerned about your welfare, it shows that you haven't really been focusing on your own welfare. And, yes, people do care. I was taking the medication. But it wasn't really the right type. I had to go under yet another medication shift, and I hated those shifts because they caused a dramatic change in my mood and thinking.

Nonetheless, the statement from Mommy really hit me that day. Just the right combination of timing, location, and personal mood brought it all into perspective for me.

"Okay, Mommy. I … I … I … um … well, you know I didn't want to upset you or anythin.' I just wanted to talk. I don't have a lot of friends. I just find that talkin' with you is real easy. Mom, I'm just ventin.' I understand, I do. The problem solvin' thin.' I wanna change. I really wanna improve. I just have too much on my mind. I just can't add more and more to my plate," I responded while drinking the rest of my Diet Coke in between pauses.

I had found an excuse while talking. I was able to obtain one and work my way out of this gentle suggestion that I perceived as a personal attack on me. I used to see every suggestion, opinion, feedback, or criticism as a very personal attack on me, an attack designed to break me down and strip me of my hard-earned achievements, an attack that had the objective of making me look like a miserable failure. It is amazing how much you can miss out from life due to this problem.

My thick, Deaf accent affected my consonant endings in my speech. When I talk to Mommy, I usually speak and sign at the same time. We both have our own sign language dialect, the one that was derived from American Sign Language. We have that unique, modified way of signing that nobody else understands. The same is true for the signing between my sister and me.

"It's okay, Josh. I know you mean well; I know you do. It's just that … maybe you just need to take some time for yourself. Get a place of your own, think about what you want to do after graduation. I mean, really think about how you interact with others. You got a few friends, but you don't have very many. Think about that. Every relationship is give and take. You have to learn to let people in. You can't be friends with people if you don't trust them with yourself. Let people in. You would be much happier," Mommy continued. It was obvious she was worn out and really didn't want to get into this type of discussion. She just wanted to have a nice day.

"Okay," I said while nodding.

I don't know why that day meant a lot to me. It was just an ordinary day, but that day was the day I had a revelation. A few words from Mom and everything made sense. I needed to do some serious thinking, so I told Mommy I'd take the car and go to the Starbucks on the beach, have a latte, and think about what she said to me.

I went to Starbucks but had an iced cappuccino instead, sitting on the beach with a towel. It was evening and not so hot. I watched the beach folks wade through the shore, looking for shells. I saw a family with their three young girls, playing in the waves that were crashing into the beach. The children were yelling, "Daddy, Daddy! Look!" while running up to the man. The father grabbed one of the youngest girls and put her on his shoulders. They all looked so happy, including the young wife.

I looked around, and the beach was beautiful. The shore was beautiful. My parents picked a great state to relocate to. Even though it gets hot in the summer, the winters are nice. The extraordinary beauty of the Floridian palm trees swayed gently, along with the trade winds. The ocean glittered under the setting sun. I felt so sad.

Then a thought came to me.

The thought came to me in such a crystal-clear way that I couldn't believe why I didn't realize it anytime sooner.

I was always alone. Every time I went somewhere, I was always by myself. I traveled alone. I liked to study alone. I liked to do things by myself. Being by myself was always hassle free, but still, something was missing. And I thought about how hard it was for me to sit through dinner with family members when I had no idea what was going on in the conversation. Anytime there was a get-together, the family loved to talk. Yes, they went really out of their way to try to include me. But it was always inevitable, the evolution of the conversation into something bigger and the shifting of topics every few minutes. And nobody in my family is a trained sign-language interpreter. It's hard to keep up. It just proved to be hard on everybody's hands, especially Mommy's. I finally realized that a few years ago. But I used to think I was not their equal because I had a disability and they didn't.

And what's even sadder is that I always felt isolated from all the other Deaf people at any functions where there were Deaf or hard-of-hearing people; never had I been able to connect to them on a level that I was so desperately seeking.

I never felt like I was ever going to be good enough for any of them, my family or those happy Deaf people. Of course, now I know that's not true. But I still felt lonely. You could be in a room full of people and be the loneliest person in the world. I looked up at the family again while finishing up my drink.

How did this happen? How did I lose most of my friends? Why did I burn so many bridges? I thought to myself.

At that moment, my whole world caved in. The realization fell upon me, one that made me see how empty my life was without relationships. And I broke down. Not just a little sniffle. I completely broke down, and my sobs were muffled by the crashing, foamy waves of the Atlantic Ocean. The tides seemed to understand my pain, and they flowed back and forth, taking my tears with them out to the deep, great blue ocean. The seagulls circled in the air peacefully around a feed spot. Nature seemed to take a moment of silence, a moment for me to grieve. The salty breeze touched my wet face. The sun disappeared to the other side, where there was land, not an ocean. It was as if nature decided I needed my space.

Even the father and his family seemed to walk away farther, giving me some space. I sat there until it was well past dusk, and I didn't leave until the ice inside my cup melted and became nothing but water. I didn't leave until my eyes were no longer red or puffy. How is it that I have seen the most beautiful things in the world, and yet feel like the saddest person in the world? How is that even possible?

The answer was simple, one that was so basic and simple that the fact it had escaped me is ridiculous. I just needed to learn how to be a good friend. I had to work on my relationships with the people around me. I had to learn how to trust people, people who were not family members. I had to face one of the greatest fears in my life: the unknown. I had to reach out into the darkness of the night outside my library and trust my instincts. And I had to accept risk, for risk is part of life.

I needed friends back in my life.

What is it like to go through a metamorphosis?

It was like a light bulb went off in my head. Suddenly, I decided that I didn't want to stay in the library all the time. I wasn't so afraid anymore. While the library was important to me, I still haven't even given the real world a try, perhaps a stab in the past, but not an immersion. But I was ready. I was now prepared to face the unknown, which was one of my worst fears. I needed to search for answers, not in the library, but out in the real world. From people. From experiences. From the species that give us the ultimate purpose for living: people. I needed to take a good, hard look at my own entire existence and finally learn things about myself that I never thought I would have ever had the possibility of doing. The revelation couldn't have come at a better time.

Indeed, the metamorphosis came at a point in my life where I was at a crossroads; I had just finished my undergraduate education at Gallaudet, and all of a sudden I found myself unsure of what I wanted. At twenty-seven years old, I had just received a BA degree, a significant accomplishment in either the hearing or the Deaf world. I had accomplished one of my most important dreams. I had made my family so proud. My résumé looked pretty good. I had made good grades.

Yet, I wasn't happy. I felt so lonely, and sadness seemed to constantly drive me into a self-induced state of melancholy and broodiness. Nothing was good enough for me. Not the school. Not the programs. Not the friends. Not even God was good enough for me. And because I felt nobody was good enough for me, I felt I was not good enough for anybody. Not good enough for my Mommy. Not good enough for my friends. Not good enough for school and a career.

I pushed so many people away: friends, family, teachers, colleagues, and acquaintances. And when I needed to have my feelings or actions validated, I sought them out. But I never seemed to quite get the reaction I was hoping for from those people. I had destroyed it at that very moment when I pushed all of these good people away by my impatience, arrogance, and unrealistic expectations. For the first time, the metamorphosis made me realize how desperately I needed happiness, and until I stopped hating myself so much, I would never know what it was to be happy. Until I found the reasons, I would continue to hurt myself, thus remaining a person in a lot of emotional pain.

Something was really wrong with me, and it had come back to remind me. I had run away from myself for so many years. A little escape every now and then is normal for a person, but when you run away so far from yourself, you become a very lost person, without a sense of purpose and direction in this world. When you abandon your identity, you lose a very vital part of your soul. I could no longer operate on the concept of "everything goes according to the church of Joshua," as one person had told me in anger once.

I did everything on my own terms. Friendships were created around unspoken terms I felt comfortable with when I was much younger. Everything had to go according to me. I was very good at manipulating people to get what I wanted. I just felt I deserved more attention and consideration. I was spoiled, to be honest. And it's easy to be spoiled if you are the firstborn.

But I think it wasn't my family that spoiled me. It was me. I spoiled myself in many ways. I carried the pretense of being Deaf as an excuse for the extra things I would ask for, a subconscious pretense. I demanded things because I felt I was entitled to some type of compensation until the Lord decided to give me my hearing back.

So deep was that feeling, I believe it weaved itself into this somewhat delusional idea that I was exempt from the many rules that society operates on. I was, of course, aware of what the rules were. But still, sometimes my behavior indicated otherwise. I acted like that anything I said or did shouldn't have been too big of a deal. I always felt, on a very subtle level, that I would be excused from it because I was Deaf. I called this assumption my "Poor-Deaf-Me Card." It is the sympathy card, the card you flash in front of someone when you find yourself in a situation that you need to get out of fast. It's the "Deaf excuse" that you use to gain an ability to wriggle yourself out of a sticky situation.

I learned a lot about relationships and trust at Gallaudet University, where the "Deaf Card" was no good; the university was full of Deaf and hard-of-hearing students, people with similar mindsets as mine. I couldn't fool anybody there. It frightened me a great deal how quickly I lost friends or burned bridges. I daresay that the biggest mistake I have ever made in my entire life was burning those bridges. But one makes mistakes. One moves on. One does not look back, only to reflect. Take responsibility for yourself and be strong. Set an example. One day, those bridges can be rebuilt.

Most importantly, I know that I am okay with my flaws and that my flaws make me unique. And that my imperfections and mistakes may help a person someday. The metamorphosis helped me understand that. The change also opened up a window that peered into my past, a past I never really thought about, nor cared about, a past with experiences that had shaped the way I perceived the world and its people.

It was time to go back in time.

BACK TO THE BEGINNING

The master rummaged through the stack of books lying upon the Venetian marble floor of his library; he was looking for his ages-old dictionary, one that had served as a very useful, valuable source of information for him. He found the huge, leather-bound book, one that would require some considerable lifting, and slammed it onto an ancient oak table. He clicked on the emerald-green overhead light; the light flickered on, illuminating the stained pages of the dictionary.

The master ran his index finger across the section under B and found the word he was looking for: *beginning*. He read the definition and immediately made a connection of the word to his life and library.

Beginning: a noun, representing the origins of something. Represents object, place, action, or concept. A specific notch in the timeline or the lifetime of an individual that illustrates the birth of something, be it an idea, memory, event, or whatnot.

The lines on the master's face seemed to have greater depth; the greenish light that was emitting from the overhead desk lamp seemed to bring them out. He had stayed up several nights in a row, for his mind could not slow down. The master was tired, yet he couldn't stop himself. He wanted to know and understand his past. It was like the dictionary read his mind, knowing exactly what he was pondering, acknowledging his deep thirst for answers. Gradually, the word at which the master was looking became brighter and brighter, no longer a black-inked imprint on a parchment paper, until it became so bright that it flooded the library with a ball of white-hot light.

Inside the library, a sudden gust of wind whipped around the master's face. Loud noises followed the wind and caught him off guard. The doors inside the library were opening, except the last door, which remained locked with a heavy, metal padlock, releasing many things. The time of yesterday had come, eager to reclaim him. It was now time. Time to go back into that place where it all started.

The wind picked up speed and whirled around the master as he could do nothing but stand still, transfixed by the incredible flurry of activity that was transpiring in front of him. The images flew across his face as he traveled back into time. Memories zoomed by, those that had shaped and created his library. The library was opening up, and memories from every single unlocked door burst out, meeting and forming a long line at the ground floor, a line that would pass him.

In rapid succession, the flux of memories rushed by the master with frightening speed and flew out the steel door to the outside world. The hands inside the grandfather clock spun backward. As the great dome, with its precious murals, disappeared, the blue, cloudy skies above were revealed, as if fresh air were just what the library needed. The library became smaller and smaller, its walls and massive columns also shrinking and disintegrating, until it finally disappeared.

During this incredible evocation of the past, the master was rapidly becoming younger and younger. His body became smaller and smaller, until he no longer could recognize himself. As the master shrank in age, his body became weaker and weaker. After a point, he could no longer stand and dropped to the floor. His neck gradually became unstable, and the master found that he could not hold his head up without lying on the floor. Suddenly, time halted. The master was now somewhere in the distant past, helpless and alone.

He was now reduced to the shape and function of a newborn child. The master lied on the floor, his eyes unfocused; he felt the cold wind beating against his skin and the cold, sterile floor. He was also searching for any sign of life. Suddenly, but surely, a pair of arms picked him up and held his neck. He immediately felt safe. Someone had picked the master up and held him close to her chest.

And there she was, with her sweet smile and beautiful voice, holding the baby. She was babbling something to him, and a toy rattle danced in front of the master's eyes. The image of this seventeen-year-old mother slowly burnt through the clear corneas of his eyes and permanently impressed itself upon his visual cortex. The warm touch of her arms and chest was forever imprinted into the library. The smile of the mother and the security it gave him built the great columns of the secret garden.

With that first memory, the library came into existence.

The smile of my mother was the first thing I could ever remember. And for over twenty years, experiences and memories would create the library to what it is today.

How does one even begin to explore his or her existence?

A nice way to begin would be to think about your first memories and experiences. How important are they to you? What do they mean to you? What type of objects or people do you see in them? Were those memories positive or negative? Could it be that those earliest memories serve as an influence on your current personality and perspective? Think about that and start from there.

You might be surprised at how significant they are.

Now, you may ask yourself in terms of recalling memory, "Well, I remember this, but it wasn't really important." But is it or isn't it? Can you sit there and tell yourself that you are who you are without really taking the time to look at events in your life, especially at the beginning? Without realizing that it might have affected you in ways you might not understand? Sure, it may be one of the oldest clichés in the world, the idea that you have to do a reality check of your soul. But it's true.

A makeover of the soul is never done overnight.

———————————————————————

There are several people I wish to thank, for without them and their role within the village that had raised me, I may have not been here today writing this story.

Let us begin with the best teacher anybody could ever ask for.

Mrs. Bales was, and still is, someone I call "Second Mom." From the first day I was enrolled in Red Oak Elementary on that fateful September afternoon of 1985, until my freshman year at Brink Junior High, she was my teacher and sign-language interpreter.

She was my role model, among many other people, and always seemed to have a serious interest in how I was doing with school. She would either praise me or chasten me for any of my performances in school and also attempted to incorporate some elements of social skills. She was also, during many years, a babysitter, always more than happy to welcome me into her home. Over the years, she had become very much a part of my family, a person that never left the room of the young Joshua. Despite the fact I've had many teachers care about me on this level, there was something special about Mrs. Bales.

Marla also has one of the biggest hearts of anybody I've ever known. She is a rare combination of a person who was strict, fastidious, caring, kind, and genuinely concerned about my future. She, especially during my rebellious years as a young teenager, never gave up on me. She would barrel me with scolding and calmly try to make me see the results of my irrational behavior when those incidents occurred (they occurred quite often during junior high school).

My favorite memory of her took place during first grade and has forever entrenched itself into the bookshelves of my library.

There was a school play staged outside Red Oak Elementary school, a play depicting the Great Land Run of 1889 of Oklahoma Territory. I was chosen as one of the cowboys that were shot at by the Native Americans. In this memory, I was asked to act out a scene, and at that age every single action had no hidden meaning. It was all real to me. Mrs. Bales explained to me that I would be dying from an arrow wound from the Native American's bow. I reluctantly agreed to die, not wanting to disappoint my new teacher, whom I thought was the sweetest person next to Mommy.

I threw myself across the bale of hay where the scene was being depicted. As the teachers made sure the fake arrow was in place and that the ketchup had achieved the desired effect of blood, I prayed and asked God to let me in heaven. I was only five and didn't know any better. And I closed my eyes, ready to die from a ketchup wound that was shot by a six-year-old Indian. After the scene was done, everybody noticed I remained motionless. Not even a peek from my eyes. I was really dead, or at least I thought I was.

Marla Bales walked over to me and tapped me on the shoulder.

I opened my eyes, and she could see that I had been crying. I told her that I really didn't want to die and asked if I could be allowed to go back inside. She laughed and explained that it was just a play. It was all just a play and that no Indians would come and hurt me. Her ability to see the humor in many situations helped me lighten up over the years as I got older. More than before, she also showed me how to persevere in face of adversity and how faith could sustain you through dark times.

What I really remember about her is that she had successfully transferred from the elementary school to the junior high, granting me the rare chance to have a teacher follow my progress all the way to end of junior high. Later on in my life, I would discover that Mrs. Bales had a hard time letting her first class of Deaf education go; she wanted to stay with us as long as she could.

It's hard for me, even right now, to explain how much I love and respect her as a teacher, friend, and mentor.

Thank you, Mrs. Bales.

Thank you for showing me the many options of my future. Thank you for taking a personal interest in my upbringing. Thank you for taking me under your wings and raising me as if I were one of your own children.

Most of all, thank you for your love and kindness. You showed me how a person can suffer and struggle, yet come out of it a stronger person; you showed me how to be a strong, new phoenix, arising from the ashes of my difficult life. I don't think I've ever really told you how much I appreciated you. I can't really put it in words; I only hope this note will speak the gratitude I have for you being in my life.

You always will have a special place in my library. And each time I see an object or painting that represents a beautiful angel, I think of you, for you showed me how to stretch and grow my own wings in the absence of sound, to fly high and far in life. Most of all, Mrs. Bales, you have showed me that I should never be limited by the physical aspect of my disability, that it knows no boundaries.

Because of you, I have succeeded in doing well in school and life.

Thank you.

Here lies yet another memory of the master, a memory and experience out of many that have altered his path in life. Without this experience, the master might have had, theoretically speaking, more difficulty living in a world where everybody could hear, speak, and communicate with relative ease.

"Hi, Josh! How are you! Come on. Time for your speech therapy!" the red-haired, young, speech pathologist said to me. She was peering from the door to her room, which was adjacent to the homeroom of my second grade class. This was at Red Oak Elementary school in Moore. The year was 1987. I looked to my teacher and waited for her to release me for one hour of fun time. She was such a welcome sight for bored, sore eyes; our therapy sessions were often right in the middle of math class, my worst subject.

"Josh, go on. Speech therapy for you!" the teacher signed to me with a smile.

Eager and excited, I grabbed my small toy and went to the speech pathologist and tried to speak in the best English possible, "Hello, Miss Huff!"

Elaine Huff looked at me and smiled.

"Are we ready?" she inquired.

"Yes!" I replied excitedly.

I have always enjoyed the challenge of speech therapy. Miss Huff (now Mrs. Hobson) motivated me with her wonderful personality and creative methods. In her adjacent office, sitting across from me, she always had such a pleasant smile on her face. I never felt forced, nor did I ever feel bored. Mrs. Elaine Hobson was firm, yet she was kind. She would pull out some materials, mostly pictures with captions below, depicting the verb, the noun, adjective, or adverb of the characters. She was quite a good artist and always knew how to explain the visual concept and the spoken word of anything I would learn. She also used sign language to create the connection for me; she truly helped me understand how to take an objective approach to the language.

She stuck with me all the way to the time I went to junior high. For me, speech therapy was a useful tool, a tool that helped me understand how to communicate with the hearing world. If you truly want to go through the training, then you have to have the desire in your heart and soul for it. This cannot be forced upon a person who is Deaf or hard of hearing. It has to come within the person, the desire. My mother simply introduced me to the idea, and I immediately seized it. Speech therapy may or may not be for every Deaf person; it is up to that person. I think back and appreciate the fact that I was given the opportunity to be Deaf *and* mainstreamed, allowing me to straddle both worlds.

Several other speech pathologists had helped me along the path after elementary school, but the bulk of the help came from Elaine Hobson. Without her and her wonderful personality that illustrated her intelligence and sensitivity, I would not be where I am. Because of her ability to engage my interest in speech therapy, what with my ADHD and all, I got the best experience out of it.

Thank you, Mrs. Hobson.

Thank you so much for making speech therapy seem less of a daunting task than it actually was. You helped me understand how the English language worked. You were patient with me while I struggled with many vowels, consonants, diphthongs, syllables, and intonation. Many of them I have mastered to an acceptable level, and it was because of you.

And thank you for letting me use sign language, to allow me to function as a Deaf person too. More often than not, there are some speech therapists that condemn sign language in their training sessions with their students. But you didn't. You allowed me to use it to make the crucial connection between two languages. You patiently corrected my speech each time I would make an error, never making me feel inferior. You were honest with me about my progress and ability; you never lied to make me feel better. You did it all with a polite, caring, tactful approach.

Many years have passed since I have last seen you.

If you don't know this already, you've had a tremendous influence on my confidence, maturity, and linguistic skills. The fact that I can understand the phonological and morphological structure of sounds and words in the language attest to the fact of your talent and qualifications. The fact that I had eagerly studied foreign languages shows that you had successfully—and I truly do mean it—incorporated the idea that spoken languages are essential for communication, just like sign languages.

You helped me realistically set my goals, and despite the fact my speech is never going to be as good as a hearing person, you had helped me learn how to properly greet people and use well-educated phrases in life and society. And you helped me accept the fact that there is always an acceptable level to work toward. And the remarks from people on how well I speak show your hard work and effort.

And I'll always remember how you used the peanut butter on the top of my tongue so it would touch the roof of my mouth in attempts to teach me how to create the *k* sound.

To this day, each time I open a peanut butter jar, I think of you. The *k* sound is no longer a scary thought for me, like it was before you introduced Peter Pan peanut butter to the sessions. To this day, I still push the top of my tongue upwards against the roof of my mouth each time I eat a spoonful of peanut butter and make the *k* sound.

You truly made a difference in my life.

Thank you.

"Hi, Josh! My name is Jo-Jo."

The year was 1990.

Into my world entered Mrs. Jolynn Ferguson, a teaching assistant at the Red Oak Elementary school. Entered a person whose youth and intelligence inspired me. Entered a person who was blunt with me about many things. Entered an incredibly loving person.

She entered the library suddenly, without announcement, without prior notice. She just popped up and forever altered something in my life. For that was the first time I've met a real Deaf adult, one who used sign language and hailed from somewhere other than the small town of Moore, Oklahoma. There are a very few people in this world who can help you make a connection between yourself and a culture that you never were a part of or even seen, a culture that was mysterious and never was fully revealed to you.

Jolynn opened that new world for me, a world that was not anywhere near the open prairies of the Great Plains, nowhere that the winds or the rains could reach. The world she opened for me was far away, which would be the world I'd eventually go to for college: the center of the Deaf culture at Gallaudet University and the full expressiveness of American Sign Language that the people there use.

Before I met her, I didn't know there could be a Deaf person who could be comfortable and happy with just being Deaf. Jo-Jo, as I call her, epitomizes that. She was young, Deaf, and proud. I also never knew how smart those people could be. The world in which I was raised was very sheltered, and she punctured a hole in that bubble and altered my consciousness.

It was as if a fresh breath of air suddenly entered into my library and revitalized my awareness. With that quick infusion of air, I was able to realize that it was indeed possible to be Deaf and happy, that Deaf people were not doomed to fail, that they were just as smart and insightful as their hearing counterparts. Farther and farther as I went along in my life, I began to realize more and more that her words rang true to my heart: Just because you're Deaf doesn't mean you won't succeed. You can do it! You can be anything you want to be! Don't let people tell you what to do! You should always listen to your heart and be proud of your Deafness. It makes you unique.

Apart from my family, Jolynn Ferguson showed me how to express myself, to form my own convictions and my own set of values. She taught me that conformity is not always the best thing for everybody and that it's not a crime to be your own person, free and independent from society's expectations. And, if you are good and kind, you will still be accepted by others.

Jolynn also helped me free the proverbial bird of the gilded, golden cage inside my library; she helped me release the bird and let it fly. The bird, because of her, has become very independent and strong. She taught me not to be afraid. She really did.

Thank you, Jo-Jo.

Thank you for taking your time and giving me the extra attention that I required as a hyperactive, sometimes confused, child. Thank you for all those lectures, advice, and activities that engaged my interest. You were someone I could always talk to, and not in the way I could talk to an actual teacher. You were the person I went to when I really needed advice or just someone to listen to. An object of fascination, you were (and still are) someone I can talk to about anything.

During my childhood years, you entered my life at the perfect moment, not a moment too soon or late. You showed me a new language of the Deaf world, and you told me about a university in a far-off place, in a city where the White House was located. You told me of exciting places, and you opened my interest in traveling far away from home. To this day, I also still think of my favorite memory of you: just the two of us at recess in fifth grade, sitting under a great oak tree, talking about life. How wonderful that conversation was! And the funny thing was that was the only time the other Deaf kids at school got into trouble and I didn't during recess! That particular conversation under that tree meant a lot to me. It was when I was able to have an intelligent conversation with you and philosophize about life in general.

There is still a blue jay out there somewhere, the bird that escaped the library, with your name on it. That blue jay was formed at that very moment you pointed at it, when it was sitting on the branches of that great oak tree where we sat under during our conversation.

In many ways, you were the gatekeeper standing by the door to the Deaf world inside my library. You were the one who created that door and its room. And you opened it when the time was right, when I was old enough yet young enough for a change. Without you, I may not have fully accepted my hearing loss and be all right with my Deafness. Because of you, I finally understood my own people: the Deaf people.

You really understood me.

Thank you.

There are so many more people who have been such an instrument to my development as a person. It would be impossible to list every single person who had an impact on me during these years. So many people I remember, be it by their names, faces, or their role in my lives, it would take yet another book to thank them all. However, I will briefly list two more influential people from the earlier years of my life.

The memory of the master is a very long one. He does not easily forget people he came into contact with.

"Josh, please calm down and do your writing exercises. Remember what we talked about? Subject, verb, predicate. Focus on that, okay?" Miss Holbert said to me during a beautiful spring afternoon in our first-grade classroom at Red Oak Elementary School.

The thing I remember most about my first teacher was her patience and her ankle-length dress and those big glasses that come along with the '80s and the frizzy hair. She was my first grade teacher, and despite the fact that it had been over ten years since I've seen her, I still remember a person who had the ubiquitous, good Oklahoman heart and someone who was cool as a cucumber. She also intervened very early in my life in terms of reading and writing. Miss Holbert had always told me that I should catch up on my reading skills to focus on writing better.

I'm not sure how it happened, but by the time I went into the next grade (where Marla Bales was my next teacher), my reading and writing skills sharply improved. Looking back at my old elementary school reports, I see how sharply the grades went up between those grades.

"Josh! Finish the reading assignment please! I know you're a very smart boy, and I am not going to accept this behavior from you. Sit down and read!" the teacher said with a very stern face.

It was September 1988 and I was not in the mood to read. I had whined and moaned, wanting to go outside; unfortunately, I was in detention for using a curse word at the teacher. I was not allowed to go to recess.

Each student needs a tough teacher. Tough teachers stay in your memory for a very long time, and their methods are far-reaching. As a young boy, I remember how much I hated this teacher, Mrs. Ohl, and it was not because I hated her personally. It was that she was a very strict teacher who seemed determined to train her students, especially in reading and math.

Underneath that tough exterior was someone who deeply cared about her students, a teacher who wouldn't lower her standards to make anybody happy. Like all the other teachers mentioned above, she stuck to the high standards; she was just blunt about it, and I got into trouble quite often with my talking back to her. However, each time I did well, Sheila Ohl always praised me and gave me rewards. She was a very good teacher because she was extremely consistent with her methods.

It took probably five times more villages to raise me than a hearing child. So much work was put into ensuring that I was progressing along on a scheduled timeline; the villagers also seemed to have a personal interest in my well-being and the security of my unknown future. They had faith in me and made sure I was aware of it. They never forgot to tell me (and the same went towards all the other Deaf children in my class) how special I was and that I could do anything I wanted to do.

They also invested a considerable amount of time in helping me tap into that pool with its scarce water and be able to squeeze gallons and gallons of water out. They taught me how to make the best of my abilities. They taught me to break barriers. They gave me everything I needed to make it in life. I would later put those tools away while I struggled with my personal demons, but those tools are back, constantly used against the test of time.

The beginning for me really took off on that first day of school of 1985 when I entered elementary school. I say this because school and education have stayed with me; it became a part of the library, and I cannot imagine what my life would have been had it not been for those people.

> They were responsible for the genesis of the librarian. Indeed, their hard work and love has ensured that the master would be able to continue on his own.
>
> He smiled, now that he had understood his beginnings in a fundamental way. In addition, looking around, the master could see that the library was now fully constructed; it was true now that the master had took a look at his past and returned to the present.
>
> He looked at the next door, where his mother was waiting inside, through the trapdoor above him. He felt better, for he had a better sense of what events had shaped his early perceptions of the world and how his library came into existence. Naturally, there were many more events, but the master was able to pinpoint those that had affected him the most.
>
> A beginning cannot be a beginning until it is recognized.

MY MOTHER, MY HERO

Inside the next room, in the dim light, the master looked at the portrait of the young Joshua and his mother.

He stood there for the longest time, pensive and contemplative. He began to have a great deal of difficulty imagining what his life would have been without his mother. Possible scenarios came into his mind, representing different destinations in life. He thought of this each time he thought of a significant person. But his mother was someone different. She was his reality, the very source of his existence and genesis. How can the master honor his mother as a good son? What laudations shall he give her? What is it that makes his mother so special?

Clearing his mind, the master approached the portrait; he placed his palm upon the mother's pleasant face. The mother's brown, soft eyes seemed to look into the master's soul. He felt her presence flowing into the room from the frozen portrait. Nobody knew him as well as his mother did. She was the single greatest influence on his life.

No contest.

She was the Rock of Gibraltar, steady and unmoving. She was the massive ship in the stormy waters of the rough seas. She was the port of safety and security.

She was but the master's friend and confidante. Above it all, she was his hero.

And she still is.

Such a profound influence on my life she is, that I cannot write about her in one simple chapter. However, as I looked into the door, I can immediately think of several things that I love about her and events that had reinforced my relationship with her. In the stormy darkness of the confusing hearing world, she was there to guide me, to educate me, and encourage me to be the strong, determined young man I am today. Her wisdom and youth also allowed her to concentrate on what was the best for me and my sister. Young in age, yet wise in years she was.

Each one of us has that person that we cannot let go of, even in death. That person will always be there for you, a person you can always trust, no matter what, a person whose opinion is extremely valuable to you. Without the approval of that person, you would feel insignificant. It may be more than one person.

That is how I am with my mother. Mommy, the one that never left me, the one that always stood by my side, even when I was wrong, the one who could make me feel like the greatest, strongest man in the world, or feel terrible about something I did wrong. Certainly, I wouldn't discredit everybody else in my family. They all were there for me and never abandoned me. But there is just that bond between Mommy and me. She was tough on me sometimes, but she never let me forget how much she loved me.

It was almost as if she was worried I would not feel loved. I wonder if she ever thought I'd be under the impression that she didn't really love me. Perhaps she needed me, too. Perhaps I was her rock out in the middle of the rough seas of life. But I know this: A gift was taken away from me, and in its place a greater gift was given to me. God had exchanged my hearing for the unconditional love of my mother, a gift that would serve a much greater purpose as time went by.

I know this because when I talk to Mommy, life doesn't seem so bad after all.

There was a long, long stretch in the timeline where Mommy was a single parent, raising my sister and me; these years, from about five years old to when I was seventeen years old, were the years that Christina and I had our mother all to ourselves.

This was a time of bonding. This was the time of strong love and conflicts. This was the time of our many road trips that only three of us took together. This was the time when it was just the three of us; we were happy and had each other. This period was also one of those where our unique friendship often clashed with her role of a mother and mine as a son. This also tested her ability to adopt the role of a father in the absence of a real one.

I was perhaps one of the most difficult children a single parent could ever raise. I was an extremely opinionated, strong-willed, and stubborn child with a love for constant pleasure (in terms of external objects, I had to have things around me, things that would make me happy). And most of all, I required constant attention. I required so much of her time.

And more often than not, Mommy gave in, granting me additional privileges in order to make me happy. I gradually learned how to manipulate her feelings in order to get what I wanted.

I was a good child, yet I was also terrible. I had a sweet side, yet when I didn't get something, the ugly, horrible side of me often erupted and created a high level of anxiety for those around me.

I often got away with it because Mommy, Grandma, and many others didn't know what to do. They must have had some guilt in their hearts and didn't want to punish me too much. Most of the time, I behaved well only after Mommy would make threats for a serious disciplining if I didn't comply. My younger sister also kept me in line. How could I say no to Christina, especially when she was just a cute little girl?

On the top of that, I made things extraordinarily difficult for Mommy whenever she would try to meet a new gentleman. I just didn't want to share her. She was so special to me, and I didn't want someone stealing her away. I was deathly afraid of losing the best friend I had during the time when I had no friends at all. *She was my mom! She's mine!* However, she stayed. No matter how difficult things became, whether it be financially, emotionally, mentally, or physically, she never disappeared. She was always there.

Looking back, I marvel at how her patience had enabled her to successfully raise two children, children who turned out very well, comparatively speaking. And I began to realize over the past few years just how much she loves me. And because of this I now have less incentive to complain and whine about life. Because of this I have a strong motivation to improve myself, to be a positive role model for my family and friends, and to act like a true leader.

I wanted to live up to my name, the name that meant "an appointed leader." I wanted to retain that strong sense of civic and familial duty, one that is expected from a strong man. Sure, it may sound sexist and chivalrous, but in my mind and heart, a great man is one who understands himself, understands others around him, and accepts challenges that would enable his family to move ahead in life and society. A strong man is someone who will provide for his family, his friends, and he is also someone who knows how to react to situations with propriety. A strong man also knows how to be kind, sensitive, and loving.

But during those years, the idea of being a great leader was distant, beyond the mountains and the rivers that were far, far away, in a place that was nowhere like Oklahoma. Woe is me! Forgive me! What guilt I experience sometimes! I was almost nothing but a spoiled, selfish child who cried or whined when he didn't get things his way! I was a child who stomped his feet and hogged the conversations. I was the child whose needs for attention completely eclipsed those of my sister. I was a child who didn't fully understand the benefits of having friends. I was one who didn't feel the need for additional friends, as I had my own mother.

This development had led to several challenges that I would have to overcome: being sociable, understanding how humans react amongst themselves, that everything is not black and white, and that having friends, networking, and accepting everybody's flaws would make you the richest person in the world. Those things would make your library rich in love, not just objects. It would not be until my new dad came into our lives that the dynamics of three people would shift to four, forever altering the family structure. And with that shift, I understood fully how hard it was for Mommy to raise a son, a son for whom she wanted nothing but great things. Dad had helped formulate a mature, adult relationship between Mommy and me several years after the wedding.

Being a fiery Aries and a passionate Sagittarius fighting each other in a cosmic battle for affection and validation, Mommy and I had many clashes over many things during this period. A cool Pisces, my sister was often the observer, shaking her head at how insane we both seemed. But with strong, loud conflicts came the powerful, sometimes overwhelming, sense of love. And that was what kept me going.

No wonder I have a very hard time leaving home. She was one of the very few people I could trust.

———————————————

Money was always tight when we were growing up.

We were certainly not impoverished by the standards of that time, but money was always a concern on Mommy's mind. I had no idea how tight money was because Christina and I always had food, clothing, shelter, and many extra things. Looking back now from our greatly improved financial position, I marvel at how incredible Mommy must have been with limited funds to ensure that we all had our things we needed for ballet and tap dancing lessons, money for field trips, and being able to receive a subsidy for those free breakfasts and lunches at the school cafeteria. We always seemed to have just enough, and we were taught not to complain; we were taught to be respectful and considerate of others, especially those who were less fortunate than us.

And most of all, she always had enough to take us on many road trips: Silver Dollar City in Branson, Missouri, South Padre Island in Texas, Zion National Park in southern Utah, summer camp in Aspen, Colorado, the Carlsbad Caverns in New Mexico, and the most memorable vacation of them all, the visit to Graceland, home of the late Elvis Presley, in the southern city of Memphis, Tennessee. Those road trips still are one of the many favorite memories of our childhoods.

I was fortunate to have been shielded away from the idea of financial struggles thanks to Grandmother and Aunt Julie, and also my uncle Dr. Robert Peters, to whom Aunt Julie is married. For some reason, during this youthful period, I never once worried about food, clothing, and shelter. No matter how hard things might have become for the single mother, we were always well provided for. There were always presents under the Christmas tree. There were always birthdays for both Christina and me. The biggest thing on my mind was doing my homework, making sure the chores around the house were completed, and going to the library to find the latest copy of a new book.

From the time I was five until my first year in junior high, never had I ever worried about money. I didn't understand fully how it was earned or how it was managed. It would be both a blessing and a downfall for me. When one does not understand the value of a dollar, one would tend to squander it away. When one doesn't understand where money comes from and how it goes out to bills, the chances of mismanaging one's funds during one's college years and thereafter increases greatly.

Yes, I was blessed in that I never understood what it was like to struggle. Maybe I was lucky that I was Deaf. I never knew what people were talking about over the phone, nor did I ever understand why Mommy would sit at the kitchen table, looking teary eyed above a modest pile of papers. I developed a somewhat unrealistic idea of how everybody in this country would always have the good American dollar, and everything would be just fine and dandy.

How stupid I was. How I lament over this! I didn't know any better. I was always staying in my happy place, impervious to the signs that illustrated the conflicts within this world.

Despite the fact that I earned money mowing lawns and doing odd jobs during my young teenage years, I never learned how to save or invest, nor did I understand that a dollar could go a long way. Instead, I spent it on movies, candy, ice cream, and things that would not last forever. I became addicted to spending money because I got the attention from the store clerks, the salespeople, and the bank whenever I would conduct a transaction. In a way, money gave me power to obtain the short-exposure attention that I was so desperately seeking. I was lonely and thought the beautiful things in my room would make me happy. But that was not always the case. Money seemed to buy me a ticket to my happy place, but I could only stay there for so long. Eventually, I had to go back to the real world.

I know this because during my college years, I squandered so much of what was granted me, and for the first time in my life, I understood the value of dollar and that one should not develop an emotional attachment to it. Money does not make a person happy. Yes, money provides comfort and security. But do not seek money to satisfy your deep need for love and affection. During my college years, after having been married for a while, Mommy finally stepped up and asked me questions about how I was managing the money I was earning. And I realized that it had become a serious problem. And out of guilt and love, Mommy had made many suggestions and proposals in an attempt to help me improve in that area. Dad did the same. Even Grandma and Aunt Julie stepped in with additional advice. It was a real eye opener. I was shocked to see how much work went into making a dollar. For the first time, truly, I had to really think about my future security. The fictional, imaginary trees were no longer growing the money that I had become accustomed to.

The point here is that Mommy was always worried about money, but she never allowed that concern interfere with our relationship. She created a safe environment for Christina and me. She went out on a limb to ensure that I only had school and chores and family interaction on my mind. She did this out of love and concern. And I don't hold anything against her. Why? Because she protected me, I was able to do well in school. I was able to have a relatively stress-free childhood until my high school years. Because of her protection I was able to develop my skills at school and be better prepared for the future.

For you single parents out there, always know that there is so much room to make errors and that some things can always be made up in the future. Just ensure that you are always there, until the very end, because your children might just need you one day, when it really counts. Always remember to protect your children, at least until high school. Don't overwhelm them with things they cannot change. Ensure that they are focused on school and their social lives. Think about what you do have. Don't focus on what's lacking in your life. Count the things that you have and life will seem less stressful. The problems of yesterday will be resolved in the days of tomorrow.

Thank you, Mommy. I didn't want to hear it, but I

learned a very important thing. Through your love and toughness, you've helped open my eyes to how my constant self-destructive behavior was affecting the present, and potentially the future, in terms of finances.

———————————————————

Another thing that makes Mommy the hero of my life is how she accepted, approached, and embraced my Deafness.

Deafness was a completely foreign concept to her; the fact that her only son would become Deaf from a virus was the very last thing she would expect to happen to her. I only can imagine the sadness she must have felt after learning that I had lost almost all my hearing. Despite the fact that the doctors warned her, this still came as a blow to her. It forced her to regroup very quickly and consult the family about what could be done.

Again, it was 1980, and there was a huge debate about those so-called treatment plans that were supposed to "cure" your Deafness: speech therapy, cochlear implants, oral-training programs, residential schools where you learn how to speak, and not using sign language. Strong and idealistic, yet pragmatic, Mommy took a really good deal of time trying to decide the best option for me. Every good mother wants nothing but the best things for her child; achieving that wish requires a significant investment, emotionally and mentally. How does a single mother even begin to comprehend the magnitude of hearing loss? How did Mommy do it?

I'm not sure, but I do know this: she went out and did everything she could to ensure that she was able to communicate with me. She wouldn't listen to specialists who claimed that the cochlear implants would cure me. She didn't listen to the oral specialists who wrongfully claimed that sign language would hinder my language acquisition skills. She didn't listen to anybody. She instead followed her heart and the advice of the family. She decided to do something that would require more work for the family than me: learning sign language and holding off the decision for a cochlear implant until I was old enough to either accept or reject the idea. Instead, she got me a pair of hearing aids because she did not like the idea of an operation so close to my brain, where things could potentially become even more problematic.

And she, out of the goodness of her heart, wanted a real relationship with me, even if that meant learning a foreign language with her own child. She wanted to be able to understand her own child and to teach the child values that had been passed down for generations and for the child to feel loved. She made some choices, hoping they would be the best choices, and played it by ear. The future was very uncertain for me. Nobody knew how I would end up. Nobody knew. Everybody ran on blind faith, praying and hoping that one day I'd be somewhat as normal as the rest of the society.

I don't believe I'm the same as everybody else. It matters not if you are Deaf or hearing. Each one of you is an individual with different experiences, and that makes you unique. But I can look at the facts and look at what I have done so far and tell you that my mother made the best decision for me at a time when I was completely powerless to make any decisions that would ultimately affect my future.

The fact is this: I'm profoundly Deaf in both ears.

I can't hear anything without hearing aids. I have a mother, a struggling single mother through the earliest years of my life, who loved me just enough to acquire a second language, enroll me in the best public schools available, and sought out other families that had Deaf children my age.

It has often been said that it's impossible for a Deaf person to learn proper English, let alone foreign languages. It's impossible for a profoundly Deaf person to succeed in speech therapy. It's impossible for any Deaf people to even have this type of writing skills, let alone a college degree. I gladly join the multitude of Deaf Americans who have succeeded in life and proved many people wrong; many of them also have succeeded in balancing their lives between the Deaf and the hearing worlds, creating themselves not one but two homes in their hearts. I just know that I always have wanted to be in both worlds because this is who I am: a Deaf person who grew up in a hearing family, a Deaf person who was mainstreamed as much as possible and can function well in the hearing world, but later developed in his heart the desire to understand and be around his own people, people that he became a part of by accident, people he felt so drawn to.

I was Deaf for a reason.

There are just so many things that Mommy had done for me. I cannot even know where to begin. I hope that I have honored my mother by moving onto the next phase of my life, toward that elusive hierarchic stage of self-actualization. But she has, in a very serious sense, basically laid out a blueprint of my library and left me with it, offering me support and advice. I took off where Mommy had thrust me at, and I took care of the rest. She made the best decision by allowing me to be a Deaf person but be around hearing people comfortably. I didn't have to burden myself with it; she carried the burden silently, hoping that one day I'd snap into place and realize all the wonderful things that had come my way.

Because of my mother, I have an unlimited amount of love and affection that seems to pour out of my heart endlessly and the burning desire to do well in life and being able to live up to my God-given name has endured for many, countless nights. And the wish to make an example of myself with both hearing and Deaf worlds has burnt on and will burn brightly all the way to my end of time, where the midnight oil would eventually run out and my body would lie itself to a permanent sleep.

You cannot be an example to others until you become an example unto yourself. Honor thy mother and thy father, by doing well in your life, and thou shall be blessed ten times over. Think of how you want to help others once you've understood yourself and helped yourself. As I approach the end of my current journey, I am seeing more and more the potential to become an example to myself; the only way to do that is accepting the fact that my Deafness will never go away. It's time to stop hiding it. Why hide in the shadows? Why hide in the library?

I have beseeched the Blue Fairy many, many times. I do not know where she is. She has never come, to this day, and probably never will. For wooden ears do not exist; therefore, they cannot be repaired.

Thank you, Mommy. I know you didn't have the power to fix my ears, but you had the greater power that nobody could ever replicate: the love that radiates from within you and the fact that you never once abandoned me. And that was more, more than enough to carry me through the sands of time, the oceans of sadness and happiness, and the winds of success and failure.

Because of you, my dearest mother, I am here.

You are my hero, just as simple as that.

CHRISTINA, MY SISTER

Closing the door behind him, the master became startled for a moment.

Standing in front of him on the railway was a huge wreath attached to the supporting beam of the specific level. Indeed, as the master walked to and peered over the railing and glanced around him, he noticed that the entire open floor of the library had been festooned with glimmering Christmas decorations. Twigs of holly adorned each level, with its prickly deep green leaves and scarlet-red berries tightly weaved around the railings. Wreaths were stocked on each level, and a huge sprig of mistletoe hung from the glittering crystal chandelier above the Italian-style reading area of the library. The fireplace of the open floor held a great blazing fire, fueled by sweet-smelling cedar logs. Stuffed stockings hung from the marble mantle. A golden, gilded nativity scene adorned the mantle top. The oil portrait above the fireplace showed a very merry St. Nicholas, with his great big belly and his jolly face, a face flushed with rosy cheeks and a cheerful disposition. A plate of freshly baked, double-chocolate chip cookies sat next to a tall glass of cold milk. Cups of hot apple cider also accompanied the meal of St. Nicholas.

The master smiled and ran down the ladder

and moved it to the next trapdoor so he could descend upon each level; the action was repeated several times until he finally jumped onto the deep-blue Venetian marble mezzanine floor. He ran toward the fireplace with a giddy, childlike expression on his face.

A great, big Norwegian fir tree, about twenty feet in height, stood in the middle of the foyer, as if announcing its importance in the wintry, icy secret garden of the library. Thousands and thousands of white lights, woven into the labyrinth of the tree branches, illuminated the Christmas tree. Delicate, crystal-colored round ornaments tinkled as a gentle breeze caressed them. Paper chain clippings in the shape of gingerbread men were strung around the circumference of the tree. Walls and walls of glimmering, tinkling tinsels hung from every available branch, creating a tree rich and laden of icy, cold beauty. A big, shining star glowed from the top of the tree; the North Star had graced the library with its presence.

Presents and presents filled the space underneath the tree; various boxes of different shapes lay against the wall next to the fireplace. A toy pony and a train set brought the Christmas tree to life. A nutcracker stood next to the pony. A new painter's easel stood not too far away. It was just like the Christmases the master knew and loved. Then something moved.

The master realized quickly that the movement came from a little blonde-haired girl who had crept from some unknown source; she was looking at the presents very carefully, as if she didn't want anybody to wake up and catch her in the action.

"Christina! What are you doing?" I whispered.

Gasping at the sound of my voice, my sister slid away the presents that had been recently stocked underneath the Christmas tree. It was Christmas morning, and Mommy was still sleeping. It was not time for us to open presents yet. Mommy had just worked a three-day shift and asked us to let her sleep in.

" Josh, ssshhh! We have to let Mommy sleep in," Christina whispered, brining an index finger to her lips, as if it were the most serious thing in the world. It was Christmas 1990, and we wanted to know what we had gotten for Christmas. We were dying to know because that year we had gotten way more presents. Mommy had done very well as a paramedic, and we had a very good year. The presents seemed to choke the space underneath, and we had a very specific wish list. I figured out what she was doing; she wanted to know what she got for Christmas. I wanted the very same thing for myself.

"Okay. I'll be quiet. So what are you doing? Hmm … ooh, I know what Mommy got you!" I chortled as I pulled a present from the tree and shook it in front of my hyper-curious sister. Her eyes widened and she immediately stiffened.

"Josh. Josh, my sweet brother." She smiled, using her innocent face. "What did Mommy get me?"

"Nope, I ain't telling you!"

"Plllleeasse! I'll tell you what Mom got you! I swear; I know exactly what Mom got. She told me not to say anything, but I really wanna know. I really need to know. I'll die if I don't know! Josssshhh, I'll tell you!"

"Okayyy … well … no. No, I can't tell you." I shook my head, enjoying the psychological torture.

"Please!" My sister's eyes widened even more, to

the point that they looked like oversized china dinner plates. Her hands were grabbing my forearms.

Feeling guilty and at the same time wanting to know what I got for Christmas, I proceeded to tell her.

"Okay. She got you this Barbie doll, and she got you the Barbie Convertible," I said quietly. Then, "What did I get?"

"You got a Nintendo. She got it for both of us, but she wanted you to think it's for you," my sister whispered.

"Are you serious? Oh yeah!" I went from a whisper to a holler.

"Josh, ssshhhh!" A voice from upstairs rang out.

"Hey! Hey, you guys! Merry Christmas!" my mother said in a sing-song voice as she marched downstairs. She looked very happy and sleepy. She had no idea we just discovered the secret inside our unopened Christmas presents. Christina and I greeted her back and hugged her as she came over to the tree. And we silently smiled without words; we agreed that we were to act surprised when we got our presents.

———————————————

I've praised my mother and my teachers. I've given credit to many people. But I still have yet to talk about someone that had such a tremendous influence on my personality and my tendency to be caring and nurturing. Because of this person, from a very early age, I've learned and experienced what it was like to be trusted with an important task: taking care of someone while Mommy was at work. Because of this person, I learned how to cook, clean, and do chores; I also learned how to keep things in order, given that I was the protector of this person during my childhood. And most of all, because of this person I understood what it was like to care for someone and love at the same time. Because of this person I knew how to have fun but at the same time be the ever-so-cautious sentinel, ensuring her safety. That special someone is my younger sister.

And her name is Christina.

"Josh! Josh, please! Slow down!" Christina whimpered while laughing.

The blonde-haired little girl whipped and zipped through the air as I spun her, holding her arms, in a centrifugal circle, her legs and feet perfectly level to the ground. Her body was but a blur, stiff and rigid. I had just increased the velocity of the spin, and I could feel Christina's hands squeezing onto mine as if she were pleading me to slow down so I wouldn't jettison her off to some scary, unknown destination if I let her go. The world was a complete blur to me; I could see nothing, and I could feel myself becoming dizzy.

Slowing down, I let my sister's feet make contact with the grassy lawn in the front of the house and let her go. With a soft bump, the little girl landed and walked around with such a wobble that she plopped down. She sat there, slumped over, groaning and giving me a thumbs-up sign, and she struggled to get up. She got up and looked dizzy but happy. Laughing like a maniac, I jumped up and down with a high-pitched, gleeful shriek, as if I were an excited monkey seeing a banana on the floor.

"More? You want more?" I said in an excited, high

voice. I loved grabbing her hands and just spinning her. I loved to entertain her.

"Me, me! Me, what about me? I wanna, I wanna!" my little cousin Rob, who was younger than my sister, piped up. He ran across the lawn to our spot, his arms extended toward me. Christina gave me an expression that indicated she had enough. I wouldn't want her to lose her lunch, as we just ate some barbecue snack food at Aunt Julie and Uncle Robert's house in Oklahoma City. It was 1993.

"Okay! Come on, Rob!" I said, putting my hands out, ready for him to grab them. And off we went, working ourselves into another well-controlled spin that would create the temporary dizziness that the kids seemed to love. Mommy and Aunt Julie were standing outside by the garage talking. Michelle, my other cousin who was the younger sister of Rob, was riding her tiny tricycle, oblivious to what was going on. Uncle Robert was outside in the backyard, where he was attending to the meat that was still cooking.

"Josh! Okay, that's enough! You're making the kids sick!" Mommy raised her eyebrows while raising her voice at me from the garage. Aunt Julie shook her head and commented that it was fine. I *was* making the children sick. But we had a lot of fun.

Christina, along with cousins Rob and Michelle, were my playmates when I wasn't around friends or peers. My sister was the playmate that played in her own little world. What an interesting world she lived in sometimes, one full of dreams and happiness, not very far apart from mine. And sometimes, our imaginary worlds would merge to make an even more interesting one. More often than not, we got into trouble, usually initiated by me, while Mommy was away. Those were my favorite memories of those childhood days with Christina, getting in trouble and wriggling out of it without Mommy ever knowing.

Josh,

For dinner, follow directions on box of mac and cheese. Watch the boiling water. When finished, mix some milk and butter with cheese powder. Be careful; don't burn yourself. Don't play around the stove.

Put hot dogs in microwave, set for one and a half minutes. Chop hot dogs, mix with mac and cheese when done. Eat dinner at 5:00 p.m., please.

You guys do your chores; remember, do the dishes, vacuum, Ajax the bathtub, and do your homework.

Grandma will stop by and check on you guys.

I will be home tomorrow evening. Don't lose your key! Please watch your sister. Lock the doors, and don't even let anybody in except Grandma. Leave porch light and TV on.

If you guys need me, tell Christina to call me with the number on the fridge. If something really bad happens, call 911 and call me. I will come right back home.

Love,
Mommy

I saw many, many of those notes while we were growing up; Mommy had to work many shifts, so that we could be well provided for. She was a paramedic, and the job required her to be away for twenty-four hours, even forty-eight hours at times. Grandma would always come by and check on us, which was pretty much every single day that Mommy was away. Those notes came from Mommy, therefore, I felt a sense of responsibility to take care of the house and my sister; I was responsible for the "home front" during those times.

On an uneventful day, while being home alone with Christina, I made some dinner as per Mommy's instructions and did my usual, dramatic dinner announcement.

"Okay, dinnertime!" I screamed from the kitchen. I often screamed and became very loud during the times we were home alone, as I never wore my hearing aids when Mommy wasn't around.

"Food's ready! Come on and get it while it's hot!" I hollered again. I banged the countertop and hollered like a maniac. "Dinner! Dinner!"

Walking in from the living room with a slightly exasperated facial expression, Christina grabbed her plate and skipped back to the living room. She then put aside the plate, sat down on the couch, grabbed the game console, and went back to playing Nintendo. Since that Christmas Day, the fabled Nintendo Entertainment System had suddenly become the central focus of many of our activities.

"Wait a minute! Wait for me!" I hollered as I grabbed my plate and rushed to her side, as I was also playing Super Mario Bros. with her. In the absence of cable television, we were very blessed to have that game to ease our boredom on many uneventful days.

Sometimes we became so bored, even the Nintendo couldn't keep us entertained. We had our own methods of self-entertainment. This scene represents one of many days where we had nothing else to do.

Screaming and laughing, I watched my sister slide down the stairs on a makeshift sled; the makeshift sled was really a mattress from those wicker bowl chairs where you're sitting on a half-bowl, basically. Sometimes we'd even take the wicker bowl off the stand and actually use that, along with the mattress, as a saucer to slide down the stairs at our old home in Moore.

Suddenly and unexpectedly, the telephone rang. We both looked at each other, temporarily stunned like deer staring at a pair of headlights. We knew that telephone call meant only two things: a) Mommy was coming back from work early, or b) Grandma was stopping by to check on us. In the time before cell phones became commonplace, our warning siren came in the form of a single telephone call from the rotary phone.

"Mommy's coming home! Mommy's coming home! Run! Oh no! Run!" Christina hollered as soon as she placed the receiver back on the wall. She had just picked up the phone and talked to someone. Immediately, we jumped to action. The chores had not been done. The dishes had not been washed. The carpet had not been vacuumed. The house was a mess. We had only thirty minutes before our mother would pull up the gravel driveway. Bumping into each other and flipping out, we ran to our chores with amazing speed. We ran around in dramatic, self-induced, sheer panic and trepidation. Hysteria usually ruled with a force during this thirty-minute period.

Thirty minutes later, we ran to the couch, sat down, turned on the television, and assumed our postures.

A few seconds later, Mommy walked in. The house was clean. The carpet smelled fresh of potpourri. The dishes glistened, having been washed. Clothes were put away. Our rooms were clean. And everything was dusted down and polished.

"Hello! You guys have been so good, I can tell! My! The house looks great! You guys are so wonderful!" Mommy said. And she went into the kitchen to eat the leftovers that we left for her. Faking two great toothy smiles, Christina and I sat on the couch and stared at our clueless Mommy, our backs straight and proud. And we winked at each other while trying to control our laughter.

We liked the dramatic effect of waiting until the last minute to see who could finish the chores first before Mommy came home. The inevitable rush that came with the danger of being caught without having done chores was irresistible. We were quite a competitive, crazy pair. This happened so many times that I've lost count. It was one of the best times I've had as a child. It was full of excitement and drama.

Drama sometimes isn't the best thing that would happen during an uneventful day. Indeed, I can remember one very specific time when, due to my boredom, I caused a slightly traumatic experience to occur for my poor little sister. Of course, no permanent damage had been done!

Singing a lullaby from *Alice in Wonderland*, my sister danced around the front lawn of the house in old Moore. I was in the backyard, near the pond that always collected in the ditch after the heavy rains that rolled over the Oklahoman plains during the summertime. It was August 1991, and there had been an explosion in the population of toads due to the excessive rains that summer.

Holding a large, glass tea pitcher, I searched and secured a great number of the depressed-looking toads. My dirty, muddy hands dug through the reefs and grasped the unsuspecting creatures and plopped them into the container. The sound of *ribbit* rang out of the container, as if the frogs were acting as a collective, protesting the unimaginable invasion and abduction of their species; the sound fell upon my Deaf ears, yet I could see their throat sacs bellowing with force. As the thick, humid air flowed along me, I skipped to the front lawn and located my target: my sister.

Ribbit. Ribbit. Croak. Crrroo-ak. The toads protested once again.

My hands held the container ever so securely. Singing indistinctly, Christina had no idea what was about to befall upon her. The Year of the Toad would soon be upon her. I slowly crept up to her from behind as she was sitting on the front concrete porch, singing something. She was wearing a lovely summer dress, and her hair had been French braided by Mommy. Mommy was across the street talking to one of the neighbors.

I held the container high up, right above the blue ribbon that had been tied onto the top of Christina's hair, and prepared to attack. Suddenly, my sister looked up to where the container was, as she had heard the mysterious language of the toads and gasped. She then let out a terrifying scream. I had turned the container upside down; the guttural toads escaped in one heavy wave, croaking and *ribbiting*. The ugly amphibians cascaded upon my sister's surprised face. And the ambush of the toads swung in full force.

Good Lord. I had never seen my sister that terrified. Wet and shivering from the slime of the toads, Christina wailed hysterically and ran toward Mommy on the other side of the road. Needless to say, I was grounded for one entire month, and I was not allowed to play with toads ever again. Even to this day, I look at a toad and think about how my sister must have felt during that terrible ambush.

Ribbit. Croak. Croooo-ak. The toads have spoken.

Thank goodness I found more constructive outlets for my boredom as I got older!

All fun and drama aside, Christina became such an integral part of my life from the day she was born to this day. Our relationship has now evolved into a mature, adult relationship, with her having been married and becoming a mother herself. Why is my sister so important to me?

I have an answer for you. Christina helped me grow into the responsible person I am today, a caring and nurturing person. Not a day goes by that I don't think or care about her and many others in my family. She had unwittingly helped me understand the importance of taking care of others and having the sense of ability to keep things running smoothly. And I see how differently she handles problems and situations; she inspires me, for she handles those with a silence that I could never understand. She is someone I look up to.

She has become someone that I love and cherish to the point that we both don't require much verbal communication. We are so close to the point that a single movement in either one of our faces gives a complete meaning to a situation or problem. With a lift of an eyebrow, I would know what she's referring to. With an expression of disgust, I'd know what she's talking about. With an expression of aghast, I'd know what she's talking about. It's just something I cannot explain.

I like to believe that's true for many of us who have siblings. We band together, united against the parental units, in a collective effort to establish ourselves apart. That might sound bold, but that's just the very nature of siblings and their relationships. We stick together, through hell and high water. Today, as I type this, I think of my sister living in North Carolina with her military family. And for some reason, I feel like she's right here with me. It matters not how long apart the visits are; she's just here in my head and heart.

She's just always here with me. I was always there for her, and she was always there for me. I'm so lucky to have a sister who understands me. And I'm so lucky to have such a strong sister who, in her own quiet way, showed me what being responsible and mature was all about.

The master looked at the young girl rummaging through the presents. He smiled, for that little girl has always been in the library; she had the innate ability to hide in the corners of the building. It was always hard to find her. Elusive, yet important she is. Christina looked up and saw the master. She smiled and got up and ran past him and disappeared behind the antique oak table.

"Oh, I see! You want to play hide and seek

again already?" The master sighed. Poking her head out from behind the table, the blonde-haired girl quickly nodded and mouthed, "Count to ten!" and disappeared.

The master laughed and closed his eyes and proceeded to count.

GRANDMA: FOOD, LOVE, AND RELIGION

The master looked up to the floors above him. The Christmas tree still twinkled with its lights.

It was time to continue. The master climbed to the floor that held the door to one of his favorite people in the world. With the familiar click and turning of the lock of the door handle, the master entered the room.

Immediately, a pleasant scent of flowers worked its way into the sensations of the master. In the background of the room, the master could hear the calming effect of opera with his hearing aid. The room was meticulously kept clean and not a single speck of dust could be found anywhere. And there she was, the brilliantly shining luminary of his life, sitting on a chair.

A classic epitome of the late Jacqueline Bouvier Kennedy Onassis, Grandma was sitting at a writing desk on one side of the room, dressed up in a Coco Chanel suit and black heels. Her legs were crossed in the classic serenity that surrounded her. Grandma was in the middle of composing a beautiful handwritten note, her senses lost in the process.

Upon hearing the arrival of the master,

Grandma gracefully put down the pen down, stood up, straightened her hair and dress, faced him, and smiled brilliantly. Classy and elegant, with an air of someone who had aged ever so gracefully, the young grandmother stood with a perfect model-esque posture and waved at the master.

The master waved back, immediately remembering his manners and the unspoken aura of propriety. Indeed, his exhausted countenance disappeared, and he put on instead a happy, respectful comportment. He then approached his beloved grandmother and gave her a kiss on the cheek and held her hands in greeting. Grandma then brought out some coffee; they sat down on the richly upholstered chairs. She and the master began to talk about the pleasantries of the day, what had passed, what weather they were having, and asking about how everybody was doing.

In her area, the walls were painted in the color of pink rose, and a scent of roses wafted from the potpourri beads by a skincare line, *Bourghese* by Princess Marcella. There was antique Chinese wooden furniture imported from San Francisco, circa the 1900s; there were Victorian lamps with Roman women and an off-white Chantilly lace cover draped over the grand, black Steinway piano. Various paintings representing the airy nuances of springtime flora hung from each wall side of the room.

Across from the piano stood an antique fainting couch, richly upholstered, circa the 1890s. The sitting chair and the writing desk were also Victorian period pieces, with their ever-so-delicate details of graceful craftsmanship. Here and there were hundreds and hundreds of books that talked about God and the gift of prophecy. Several books discussing the topic of dream interpretation also were visible. A television set stood not too far with its shelves full of compact discs of the great Christian evangelists (namely Joyce Meyer, Gregory Dickow, Billy Graham, Joel Osteen and many others) and some of the greatest tenors in the opera world: Julio Iglesias, Luciano Pavarotti, and Andrea Bocelli. A framed photograph sat on the piano, a picture taken during Grandmother's recent visit to the Holy Land in Israel; a videotape also stood close by, one that had documented one of her most cherished lifetime experiences. A language instruction book and tape in Hebrew also sat there, one that was for the master.

It was like stepping back in time, back to the time where everything was cherished: the idea of proper self-presentation, the idea of taking one's time, the idea of romanticism and classicism. Back into the time where the simplicity of one's life was not burdened by the hustle and bustle of the modern period. Back to the days where people took the time to talk to each other with a smile.

The master always felt relaxed in this room. It had been a long time since he had really visited with Grandmother. But she was always there and always happy to have him back, no matter how far away the master had been or how long he had been absent. And only very recently had the master begun to revitalize his relationship with his beloved Grandmother. On the other side of the room was the kitchen.

The kitchen, with its memories and history that had become so entrenched into the personality and tastes of the master, beckoned to him. From the sitting area, the master could see an entire plethora of culinary delights. On the counter stood also tons and tons of sweets, for the master had a sweet tooth. There were éclairs, strawberry shortcakes, fudge brownies, pumpkin pies topped off with whipped cream, chocolate chip cookies, apple and peach cobblers, vanilla ice cream with rainbow candy sprinkles, popsicles with their simple yet exciting flavors, and cream cheese Danishes, complemented by the deeply infused French roast cup of coffee.

The grandmother, with her regal and classic beauty, looked back at the master, and smiled. She knew the master was hungry. Out of love, she went straight to the kitchen and fifteen minutes later she called the master to the kitchen. The master approached the kitchen counter and smiled, for Grandma had handed to him his favorite food: a plate of grilled cheese sandwiches and a glass of milk. She had showed her love for the master by ensuring a steady flow into his stomach. The master and his grandmother said a quick blessing; he then chomped down on the sandwich and glugged the milk until it all but disappeared. Grandma smiled and sat across the counter from the master and, with a lovely posture and an air of classicism about her, drank her coffee quietly.

She was happy; her grandson came by to visit her. The master almost never knew it, but each one of those visits became more and more significant to her as time passed by.

Everybody in this book, up to this point, is so important to me. Everybody has his or her own unique contribution to the library of mine. I'm very happy to say that Grandmother had brought a type of love that can only be established between a child and his grandparents. I am so lucky to have her in my life.

I never knew what it was like to be hungry. As an American that feels guilty, I have to confess: I never understood how lucky I was until very recently. Not a day went by that I didn't have a meal. Never. And Grandma made sure of that. To this day, each time I think of Grandma, the very first thought that flies to my head is that ever-so-available plate of grilled cheese sandwiches, a bowl of tomato soup, and a glass of milk.

Indeed, every day after school when Mommy was at work, Grandma would always ask me a question. A question that, even as I approach my thirties, still means a lot to me: Josh, are you hungry? Do you want Grandma to make you something to eat?

The staple comfort meal had become so much a part of me as I became older. Certainly, Mommy made sure I ate. Christina made sure I ate. Dad made sure I ate. Even Aunt Julie made sure I ate. I was extremely well-fed. But Grandma had always been the one that went out of her way to ensure I had food in my stomach. To her, the ritual of having a proper meal was very important, and she would not be satisfied until she was certain that I had enough to eat. It's as if she was, and still is, the personal Julia Child of the kitchens of our family and my library; there is nobody else that can cook quite like Grandma. We all strive to bring our cooking abilities to her level.

This was especially true for the holidays. We all love her cooking at Thanksgiving. How extraordinary her food always tasted! Thanksgivings were always my favorite time to spend with Grandma, for we often went over to her house for the holiday. Despite the fact that in recent years we've shared locations for Thanksgiving, I still cherish the memories of our delicious feasts and how we all would be packed into that dining room inside the simple, suburban ranch house in Moore, Oklahoma.

———————————

There is also something else about Grandma that everybody should know: She always made sure everybody was included. And she was always acutely aware of how I would feel left out sometimes during the holidays. It wasn't that anybody didn't care. It was just the nature of my Deafness, and nobody was a trained sign language interpreter. So, from early on, she did something very special for me, especially during my childhood and teenage years: allowing me to lead the prayer for Thanksgiving. Grandma doesn't know it, but that was the most important thing she ever did for me during the holidays.

It wasn't the food I wanted. It wasn't the birthday presents I wanted (my birthday is always very close to Thanksgiving). It wasn't the dessert I wanted. It was attention. I wanted attention so much, and Grandma was one of the people in my life that gave me attention, along with Mommy, the teachers, Aunt Julie, and many others. She understood my desperate need for validation and confirmation. Each time anybody gave me attention, I felt important and special.

Grandma recognized that without a doubt; indeed, she became even more special to me when she asked me a question that would forever cement my deep respect for her as my grandmother.

"Josh, would you like to say the prayer?" Grandma inquired.

"Uh…Uh, sure," I said, completely surprised. This was the first time she had asked me a question like this on Thanksgiving Day. It was Thanksgiving 1991, and I had been just asked to recite a prayer for the feast. A sensation of nervousness washed over me. An important task, no exaggeration, had been handed down to me. It was as important as carving the turkey. It took me a while to get my thoughts collected while everybody at the table stared at me politely.

Excited, yet nervous and surprised, I said to everybody, "Yes. Okay. Are we ready?"

I was eying everybody for visual confirmation, and I turned my hearing aid back on.

All heads turned toward me, as to wait for me to begin.

Bowing my head and using sign language at the same time, I spoke out in very broken English, trying my best to recite the Lord's Prayer, in an affected Deaf accent:

> Ower Fader, who art in heven,
> 'Allowed be thy Name.
> Your kingdom come.
> Thy weel be dunn
> Here on erth as it is een heven.
> Geeve us these day ower dally braad
> Und foorgeev us ower trespasses,
> As wee foorgeev those who trespass to us.
> Und sumethin' 'bout tempt—I looked over to
my Mom, and she nodded

But dee-liver us fram eeeveeel.
Ah-men.

Everybody was so polite. Mommy smiled while bowing her head; Grandma nodded with her eyes closed; Aunt Julie and Robert did the same. Uncle Todd and the cousins Rob and Michelle smiled at me curiously. How different my speech was! How interesting was the manner in which I used. Nonetheless, as good family members, not a single one of them feel embarrassed or ashamed for my awkward speech.

"Amen," everybody said in unison after I finished the prayer. Many looked at me and smiled as if they were proud of me. They had just done the best thing they could do to a Deaf person: accepting me for who I was and appreciating the fact, not the way, I said a prayer. To think that my family would be proud of me, a Deaf person with seemingly limited potential in life, for showing the love for our Lord the God, meant so much to me. It was such a huge boost to my fragile self-esteem, and I eagerly looked to the Thanksgivings thereafter.

Nobody knew this but every year right before Thanksgiving, I would practice my prayers with my speech therapist so that I could better please my family. I wanted to please my Grandmother. Nothing was more important to me than having the pride of the family in me. Each prayer was expressed better, for my speech gradually improved over the years. Some Thanksgivings I was too self-conscious, especially during my teenage years. But I still remember how so very kind my Grandmother was when she allowed me to lead the family in grace for the very first time.

That was a very special birthday present to me, and

I still count that Thanksgiving as one of my favorites. I was about to turn twelve, and because of Grandma's love and kindness in making that specific request, I felt like a full-grown adult, ready to be part of the grown-up table.

And I was welcomed with open arms.

It didn't matter how Deaf I was. It didn't matter how spastic I was. It didn't matter that I had ADHD or mood swings. It didn't matter how well I spoke. None of that mattered. She wanted me to feel special.

"You are very special, Josh," she would always say to me.

And hearing that from the matriarch of the family is all I ever need, even to this day. Each time she says that, I have to fight back tears because it overwhelms me that someone would go out of the way and tell me that. And not only telling me that, but projecting that specific declaration with genuineness, respect, confirmation, and love. I needed someone other than my own mommy to tell me that, and she never failed to say this year after year. Certainly, Mommy never failed to say the same; Mommy still has been first and foremost the strongest supporter of me, one that always told me how blessed I was, how lucky I was, and how special I was.

But it's always nice to hear it coming from other people, you know?

It's actually very hard for me to describe in words how special Grandma is to me.

There are three other things about Grandma that make our relationship a special one: a) the fact that she's a grandmother; b) the fact that she had helped me understand the importance of being proper and polite toward others; and c) her love for God.

Every one of us who has a grandparent can almost always say the same thing. The relationship between you and your grandparents is different than that between you and a parent. It's special and unique. I don't think I could explain it any better. It's just different and special. Again, I wouldn't discredit anybody in my family.

Indeed, while Mommy had the drive and energy of a young woman and kept me energized, Grandma possessed the wisdom of an older, more experienced person. Her experience and the way she dealt with situations inspired me to do the same. I had watched her from an early age and marveled at how she handled things with grace and dignity. She is not one to complain. She is not one to speak negatively about others. She was always there to guide everybody through life. And her love for God amazes me.

And I have watched many, many people mistreat her. People disregarded her feelings, her experiences, her wisdom, and her true love for God. I marvel at how incredible she was, just like Mommy, when she dodged those arrows and stones with an incredible precision that only comes with age and wisdom.

From time to time, I have seen those fleeting looks that fly across her face, looks of loneliness and sadness. For so long, I have sat silently and maintained composure whilst observing her. I know she is my grandmother, but she is also a woman, one that had seen much out of life. I see a woman who is perhaps, in a very small way, afraid of being discarded and forgotten, like many of her peers.

That will never happen. I'll personally make sure of it.

That's right. Don't you fret, Grandma.

Don't worry, Grandma. There is no reason to be sad. We all are always going to be here for you. And if it ever happens, I'll take you into my own home, shower you with love and affection, and make sure you deserve everything that you've worked ever so diligently in your lifetime. We may not say this everyday, but you are the nucleus of this family structure, and we cannot imagine it without you.

In this country, the idea of becoming old is terrifying. I admit it. I soon will say good-bye to my twenties and enter the new realm of the next phase, the thirties. In this country, the older you are, the less valuable you are. That has always been such an incredible disappointment to me, for you do not decline as you age; you become better with age. Dr. Robert Peters, my uncle and dentist, always told me this: With age comes wisdom. I admire my grandma for I have seen many of her peers, both strangers and friends, carry themselves with misery, unhappiness, and defeat.

But not my Grandma. She is so far from a poorly prepared dish of raw chopped liver; she has always shown me the possibilities of aging gracefully while retaining the youthfulness in your heart, coupled with unparalleled wisdom and a love for our Lord. She showed me how, in spite of things that come at you, one could create an invisible force that would keep the person emotionally and mentally (physically, too) intact, forever and ever. She inspires me so much by showing me that you can be old, yet be happy and strong. Strong like a steel magnolia. Strong on the outside, yet soft and sensitive inside. That's my grandmother.

She doesn't know this, but not a day goes by that I don't think about her and her well-being. Why is that so?

Again, I have never been the one to follow the general, negative trends of this country. I have an enormous amount of respect for Grandma, and naturally, as a good, dutiful grandson, I always am exhorted to try and be the earthly guardian angel of her. I often call the angels of Lord to watch over her.

Grandma had protected me and everybody else in the family through prayers and faith. How could I not return the favor? It's the Christian thing to do. I like to think that she had preserved the family through her prayers; we all have our health and happiness because one way or other, her prayers had always created an umbrella of protection over us. It's still hard for me to find the right words to explain my relationship to Grandma and how so very special she is to me. But I can say this: Grandma is one of the most important people in my life.

No contest.

She is one of my brilliantly shimmering stars in the starry night skies. She is to me as Jackie O was to America. She is to me as the sun is to the glittering Atlantic Ocean. She is to me as zephyr of the west is to the east. Just like Mommy, she is also the rock; she is always there to guide me through the trials and tribulations of my life.

Have you no idea how special you are to me, Grandma? How I want to please you by showing you that even today young people can have just as much class as your generation? How I care for you and how I much look forward to our weekly Sunday drives to church? And how, as each year passes, much more I cherish you? That the more I know you, the harder I can imagine life without you? Would that I could explain in more intricate terms how important you are to me. Would that I, as a writer, could find a better way to illuminate you?

I wish for the world to see how special you are to me. How your faith and love in your family have always rewarded you and all of us. How your love from the snows of yesterday had quenched the family's thirst for love and guidance today. How you've taught us to hold our heads high and take the higher roads in troubling situations.

It is often a difficult task to describe the importance of someone in our lives. I only hope I have expressed my love, affection, and respect for you in the best terms possible. Thank you for being the guiding light of the family, and thank you for never giving up on me. Thank you for accepting me in spite of my Deafness. I hope I have made you proud of me, in spite of my hearing loss.

I am so lucky to have you in my life.

I love you.

Mommy and me at the Snowmass Mountain near Aspen, Colorado, before going to summer camp. 1994.

My first dog, Casey. He was my best friend from 1989 to 1997.

Christina and me hanging in my bedroom, 1986.

Dad and me decorating the Christmas tree, 2003.

Mom, Dad and me at my first prom, 1997.

Dad, Christina, Mom, me and Grandma at our condo in Florida.

My sister's new baby, her husband Ryan and the family
members, 2006.

Mommy, me, and Eddie (my biological father), November
28, 1980. This was my first birthday.

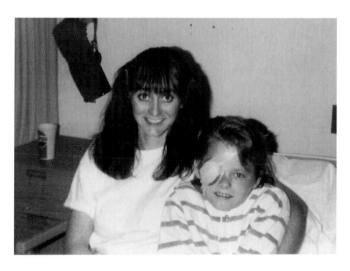

Mommy, me, and Eddie (my biological father), Christmas 1979. This was my first Christmas picture.

Mommy and me at a hospital, after my serious eye injury, 1990.

*The Deaf Gang: Joani Russell (Osborne), Joshua Dowling,
Daniel Dickens, Tara Anderson, Heidi Sills and Victoria
Hamm. Sixth Grade at Red Oak Elementary School.*

*Jolynn Ferguson and me at our college graduation from
Gallaudet University, 2005.*

Grandma and me, Christmas in the early 80s.

Christina and me, 1988.

Daniel and me monkeying around at recess, 6th grade, Red Oak Elementary School in Moore, Oklahoma.

Julie and me, Christmas 1986. My favorite aunt, ever!

Julie and me having our traditional lunch on the riverside in Melbourne Beach, Florida.

The only photo I have of Kristen Rogers, an interpreter and a friend. I will miss you, Kristen.

Mommy holding me in front of the mirror, much to my delight, early 1980s.

The flagship photo of Mommy and me; to this day, this re-mains the favorite photo of mine. Taken in 1985.

My first niece, Julianna, whom I will always cherish as my first one, 2006.

Me, Dad, Mommy and Christina. Thanksgiving, 2002, in Indian Harbour Beach, Florida.

My favorite girls next-door, the Anderson girls. Along with Mommy, Christina and me are Tara, Sonya, and Rachael Anderson.

Favorite picture of me and great-uncle Todd: Christmas, 1989.

Mommy, Christina, Grandma and me on Christina's birth-day, 1987.

Grandma and me at Mommy and Dad's wedding, May 1998.

Mommy and me at her wedding, 1998. This was the happiest day of her life.

Just another typical summer day at the Oklahoma City Zoo with my sister in the summer of 1988.

BOY, INTERRUPTED

The master remembered a room he had skipped while looking into other rooms recently: the room representing his life after childhood. He didn't like this room for it was a room that revealed many things that had battered the master.

Sighing, the librarian knew he had to go. He picked up the ladder, which had been lying on the floor, and did the usual ladder-trapdoor-floor thing until he arrived to the platform where the plaque read "Interruptions."

He opened the door after unlocking it with the antique golden key and entered.

My entire life, up to the age of seventeen, had been a series of constant interruptions; those interruptions were usually related to a physical accident or issues with my mental health. It was not just the hearing loss that had led me into the inevitable realm of depression; it was a gradual progression of accidents, catastrophes, and clinical problems. While this chapter discusses several things that had happened to me during my childhood, most of the serious things had occurred from the time I was in fifth grade to the last year of my high school experience.

First, let us look at an example that is very deeply

tied to the two major events that had traumatized me in a way where I had a very hard time recovering from. These events also prevented me from entering in any type of contact sports (I've always wanted to understand and play rugby, lacrosse, tennis, and basketball). It also exhorted me to dig deeper into my library and cultivate a persona in the fine arts world, especially when it came to higher education.

———————————————

April 1990
It was springtime, a wonderful one, those types of spring days that have the right kind of temperature, humidity, and what have you. Oklahoman springs are wonderful. I was sitting on the porch of our house, off the old street of Broadway and downtown Moore, Oklahoma. Christina, my younger sister, was playing outside with a girlfriend.

As the habit for those warm days that came with the first kiss of the April sun, my sister and I would go outside to play or read; Mommy would encourage us to get out of the dusty house and enjoy the fresh, spring air. Indeed, I did most of the reading while my lovely sister always seemed to have a friend or two over. Those were the best memories I have of me and my sister, the times when we both didn't have adult responsibilities.

They were playing outside, and I was engrossed in the plot of a book. I was sensitive to any sudden changes in the environment, visually, as the eyesight of a Deaf person is especially acute. And something darted into my field of vision. I let out a sudden gasp and shielded my face with my arms in less than a split second. My book fell to the ground, which I had been reading.

"Oh, I'm so sorry, Josh. Are you okay?" my sister inquired, a worried look on her face. She had accidentally thrown something in my direction, toward my face, while aiming for her friend. The object hit my arms and dropped straight to the ground. Still breathing slightly hard, I let my arms down.

"I'm fine! You scared me," I replied in a high, aggravated voice while signing to her. I continued while rubbing my forearms, "I really thought it was going to hit my face! I can't deal with that, you know!" My sister stood there with her mouth wide-open and wary eyes. She didn't know how to react. The football lay on the ground, motionless. It had barely avoided a head-on collision with my face where my arms had blocked it.

"Sorry. I didn't mean it," she said in a quiet voice as she walked over to the football and picked it up. She continued playing with her girlfriend, but she made sure they were at an acceptably far distance. I could tell she felt really bad.

"It's okay! It's not you. It's just me. I love you." I smiled at my sister, who seemed a little bit frightened by my sudden, furious reaction. I continued, "I'm going inside to finish my book, okay?"

She nodded her head and continued playing with her friend. I walked into the house, slamming the screen door behind me.

There was a serious, underlying reason why I showed little tolerance for those types of situations. It was just that I hated it. I still hate those situations, where flying projectiles seemed to possess the high potential of injuring any area of my face. The reason was inevitably linked to two memories that account for my apprehension of flying objects: an accident involving my right eye and another one involving my upper frontal teeth.

Those two accidents have shaped me so that I cannot accept anything flying at my face. Being an accident-prone young boy with a hearing impairment is not something I would wish on anybody.

I've already lost my hearing. I didn't need to lose yet another one of my remaining senses.

———————————

The first one I can remember occurred in late March of 1990, in Moore, Oklahoma, at our old house on N.E. 2nd in Old Moore.

The twittering of the birds tickled the amplifier of my hearing aid. The sun was shining, and the air was cool, yet warm. A wind swept across the prairie, and the new buds on the tree branches quivered. Spring had arrived, yet winter had not left. Mommy and my sister were inside the house, doing some spring-cleaning. Outside, I was on the field, as our house was near the railroad tracks.

I was sitting on a go-cart, which was propped head-on against a tree; the engine had gone out mysteriously. Mommy had bought me a go-cart, as I demanded one for my birthday a few months earlier. I took off my sun-glasses and put them down on the passenger seat and climbed out of the go-cart. I decided to check the motor to see if there was anything out of order. Everything looked in order. The motor looked fine. The gas tank was half full. The oil was fine. Everything looked just fine. I proceeded to grasp my right hand around the starter piece and prepared to give the engine a start. I gave the starter a quick, hard jerk, as you would for a lawnmower.

Then it happened.

A piece from the motor burst out and flew straight into my right eye.

As it penetrated the cornea of my right eye, I dropped the starter piece and immediately released a blood-curdling scream. The cord retreated back into the sinister motor. It had committed the perfect crime and got away with it. There would be no punishment. There would be no justice. The nerve-rattling scream carried itself over the railroad tracks and in the other direction; it also carried itself past my house and the neighborhood. The screaming, accompanied by painful cries, never stopped. I could not stop screaming, especially when I saw blood coming out of my eye. I could see the scarlet color all over my hands. I stood there, completely in shock, and my screams went unanswered. It was as if I were transported out of my consciousness and couldn't control myself anymore.

Pulling the foreign object out of my eye, I cried even louder. I couldn't believe it was happening. It hurt so badly. More blood gushed out of the corners of my damaged eye.

Against the cool March wind, I stumbled across the watery ravine that separated the house from the field and kept screaming, hoping someone would come. The walk to the house was the longest walk I've ever known. Yes, the house was in my sight, but it seemed that the closer I got, the farther away the house was.

"Mommy!" I screamed as I burst inside the house. A filthy mixture of mud, sweat, and blood covered the entire right side of my face, and the front of my shirt was drenched in blood.

I frantically searched the house for Mommy. She was drying her hair with the blow dryer in the bathroom. The loud noise had concealed my cries for help.

She suddenly turned off the hair dryer as she saw me walk into the bathroom door. Her facial expression immediately changed. Christina also had popped back into the house. She was mortified at what she saw.

I lurched into the bathroom with my arms extended toward her, screaming, scratching her, and weeping. I dropped to the floor and nearly passed out. She grabbed me, hoisted me up on the closed toilet seat, and being an experienced paramedic, she asked me many questions, trying to get some answers.

"Josh! What happened? Talk to me! Let me look at you. Oh my—" A string of expletives escaped her lips, those that one would make when someone is deeply panicked and shocked. She examined my face, and she immediately grabbed me, picked me up, and carried me out of the house. We were going to the ER.

The doctors ran a battery of tests, CAT and MRI scans, and the hospital stay lasted for a good week. While they were able to save my eye, the damage was done. I just had lost my sight in my right eye. It would never be normal again. A detached retina and a split pupil is not something that can easily be repaired. More now than ever, my other senses became extremely valuable to me from that point on.

Spring 1992

The second accident was perhaps not as serious as the first one, but it had further cemented the idea that I should avoid any type of slippery surfaces, sharp corners, and that I should always eat three square meals a day, end of discussion. The aftermath of this particular event resulted in many trips to the dentist's office.

"Hello? Hey." I said.

I had raised my hand, hoping to get the teacher's attention. I was not feeling well and there was an unsettling feeling inside my stomach. We were at Brink Junior High in Moore, Oklahoma. I was in seventh grade, and we the classmates were sitting on the floor of the library, listening to a presentation. It was early morning, and I had arrived late. I missed my usual course of breakfast and was not feeling well. I felt like passing out. Something was wrong.

"Yes, Josh?" the teacher signed to me.

"I really need to go to the bathroom," I signed back to her. My face was pale.

"Sure. Are you all right? You look terrible," she responded back to me.

"I'm fine. I just need to go to the bathroom. I'll be right back," I said weakly.

I stood up and felt a wave of dizziness wash over me. I turned and exited the library into the hallway. Someone had recently cleaned the floors with wax. I proceeded to wobble down the hallway, knowing that, at the intersecting hallways, the bathroom would on my left. I walked and all of a sudden I fell forward. You know the feeling that you experience when you take a dive off a board into the pool? Well, that was exactly what happened to me. As I walked, I sped up, and literally dove to the floor, my body limp like a sack of bricks. My shoes had given way to the slippery surface.

Crack.

The floor hit my teeth. It broke my two frontal upper teeth as I slammed my face on the cold, hard surface. The fractured pieces shot out and disappeared, blending into the colors of the floor. It would take four teachers and a principal a long time before they could find those two missing teeth. Still weak from the mysterious illness, I lay limp on the floor, barely conscious of what had suddenly occurred. Hands were pulling me up, trying to get me to walk upright. I could barely walk without feeling like passing out. I was put into the principal's office while a telephone call was made to my mother.

I had contracted some kind of virus or bacteria, and I had just lost my two upper frontal teeth. And I was entering my adolescence years, and I was already dealing with fundamental issues. Did I need this?

I was transported to the ER, which seemed like a second home to me after having broken an arm due to a typewriter falling on me, suffering a dog bite when I was six, not to mention the eye accident, and one that just had happened. I sat there in shock as doctors examined me, drew blood, and tried to figure out why I was so nauseated. Then they proceeded to discuss with Mommy about a procedure that I would soon physically block them from doing.

"Whas is das ding?" I said in bad speech, as the teeth were missing, and I had a hard time pronouncing the *th* sound. Inside my mouth there was an ugly gap with the crooked, serrated edges where the fracture had occurred. There were no buck teeth to press the tongue up against to make the *th* sound. Or the *t* sound. A medical resident, according to Mommy, had just entered the room with a sharp object. I had never seen something that large. I never liked needles and still do not like them.

"Josh, listen to me. This is a needle, and they think you may have meningitis again. They really need to do a spinal tap," my mom signed to me.

"A spinal dap? Wait a minnnn…You mean dey're

gonna puh da ding in my *back*? No way!" I hollered. My face was crooked with anger and indignation.

"Josh, just let them do it," she coaxed.

After a great deal of thinking and griping, I gave them the go-ahead. I sat there, my hospital robe open, exposing my back, and squeezed my mother's hand tightly. And there it was.

A gigantic needle with an empty vial, ready to greedily suck the precious fluid out of me, glistened under the fluorescent light bulbs. I watched as it disappeared from my peripheral vision, and I turned to my mother's face. She was watching it move, and suddenly her eyes shifted to me, her face laden with a grim expression. My instincts kicked in.

Releasing a terrifying scream, I screamed and turned around, visually located the needle and pushed it away, and screamed bloody murder. In the moment, I also kicked and pushed the doctor away with my powerful legs. The resident fell back and crashed into a cart that was sitting behind him.

"Noooooooooooo! You're nod gonn' hurd me! You don' know whaddya doing! You're nod gonna pud me in a wheelsshhhhhhhhhaaaaaaaaaair!" I screamed with multiple expletives shooting out of my mouth like a long, uninterrupted series of firing bullets.

The medical resident got to his feet, completely flabbergasted at this horrific display of preadolescent anger and ran out of the room.

"Ged da hell away from me! Are you insane? Ya, da's right! Run away! You're so dupid!" I continued screaming, my mouth struggling to form words. My mother very quickly stepped outside, as this situation was perhaps too much for her. And all the screaming had caused me to lose energy again. I sat back on the bed and nearly passed out again.

I didn't have meningitis, but nobody ever knew what was wrong with me. I wouldn't let them stick that thing in me. Nonetheless, I felt much better after a good fortnight in the hospital and home. From that point forth, I have tried to never miss breakfast, or at least never go without three meals a day. I still cannot miss a meal to this day without feeling apprehensive. I'm afraid I'd become dizzy again.

"Josh, keep your mouth open. I'm going to make an impression of your upper row of teeth. We're gonna get you some nice new teeth. Now, keep your mouth open; this will be hot," my uncle Robert, the dentist, said. He had removed his mask so I could read his lips, and now the mask snapped back, covering his mouth. He went straight to work, his focused eyes burning intently upon the task before him. Gasping as the huge impression tray invaded my mouth, I sat there thinking about what a hellish nightmare I was being subjected to.

It was a month later, and I had come back to my uncle's office for what seemed like the thousandth time. I was anxious to get my permanent crowns so that I could have some type of a normal smile. I was so sick of the horrible resin-based temporary teeth. It looked like nothing like anything I've ever seen in a person's mouth.

First, my ears were burnt out. Then I get an eye damaged. Now this happened to me. Will it ever end? The accidents, the torture, the endless parade of catastrophes that seemed to follow me everywhere?

A few months later, I looked at my new crowns. They looked real, and I was thankful for my uncle. He had done an excellent job. Dr. Robert Peters really helped me out when I needed it, and I'm forever in his debt.

Perhaps that's why I'm so obsessed with smiles. After that I started to really appreciate smiling and showing a set of nice, clean white teeth. You have to lose something in order to appreciate it more, truly.

Everybody has secrets. Some secrets should remain secrets. Some secrets may help others. I will tell you a secret. And the fact I'm putting it on a written medium shows how much this experience had opened my eyes to life and the joy of being alive and how important I feel it is to share this message.

My secret is this: I almost ended my own life during my senior year in high school. Without intervention from Mommy, I would not be here telling you this story. Threats, thoughts, or an actual act of suicide is no joke. The elements that push a person to this scary area often are overlooked. It is often not taken seriously.

I rejoice in the fact that my life has not been interrupted by death. It's almost as if I wouldn't allow myself to be defeated, not after what I'd been through.

Let me present you the most difficult experience of my entire life. And how I came out of it intact.

You know, I like to think I've always been a good student in school. People tell me I was. And I've always tried to do well to please everybody. I was on the honor roll. I was a member of the National Honor Society. I was a part of the Latin and French club. I had a part-time job and a car. I kept my GPA above 3.0 and tried to participate in extracurricular activities. I was doing pretty well for a Deaf student in a mainstream school.

I wanted to fit in. I wanted so badly to forget about problems that had been persistent, persistent to the point that they had formed a cancerous tumor in my psyche. It was not until my senior year that the tumor in my psychological well-being finally overtook me and nearly drove me to suicide. How did this happen?

This will be perhaps a very important passage in this book, a very important lesson, a lesson that could help you identify some problems before they become those that would take a lifetime to control.

———————————————————

The physical accidents were when it all started; the depression came afterwards. Combine that with my ADHD, it proved difficult for me to find a way to appropriately channel my anger that came from being depressed. While I recovered from the accidents, my soul did not.

For years after the accident, for some reason, I felt disillusioned. Life was no longer simple or happy. In addition to dealing with the issues that enter life when undergoing puberty, these things had become so bad that I had become an expert in trivializing problems. I become a master at concealing. I became so good at putting the problems inside the rooms of my library that I actually, after a period of time, failed to recognize the underlying causes of my thinking and behavior. I began to acquire an outward appearance, one of a proper young man, while inside I was screaming for help and affirmation.

So bad the depression became that it aggravated my clinical conditions: ADHD and borderline and addictive personality disorders. Before puberty none of these clinical problems were even that serious. Before the accidents, I felt that these problems weren't really too serious and never really interfered with my ability to be happy. But that changed after the interruptions. And because I never understood these disorders, I began to change in terms of behavior. I became cold and critical of others around me. I put God aside and stopped going to church. I pushed people away. I became socially isolated. And I lost interest in family functions. I turned to food for comfort. I turned to books and education for comfort.

I no longer knew how to deal with my own problems; instead I buried them under the mat. Something was really wrong with me. And it remained inside me for many years, until the day I had my nervous and emotional breakdown. At seventeen years old, having a breakdown is a very scary thing. It happened after I had finally declared to Mommy that I wanted to take my own life and that was when I actually meant it. At seventeen years old, I was sent to the institution to get some professional help.

I disappeared from school for most of my senior year. People wondered where I had gone off to. People would inquire about me, but the answer was always this: he has an illness and he needs to recover. He is being home-schooled and everything is fine.

Yes, I recovered. It was a breakthrough, my experience at the medical center during my senior year. It had really helped me. But there was still just quite some work to be done. Quietly, I continued my help. I was very afraid to talk about this to others. The stigma was so great. But not anymore. I can talk about this. I was put on medication, the first of many ineffective series of medications.

Today, I finally have found my right combination of medication. *Paxil* has increased my ability to be calm and sociable. *Buspar* has helped control my anxiety. *Adderall* has helped me maintain the critical element of focus and self-discipline.

I have finally found the right combination, and after ten years of professional therapy, I've finally been able to understand how to analyze myself. And I am now in a position to offer my experience and advice to others. I know I'm only scratching the surface here, but these are the facts, and I will go into these facts more in detail in what I hope to be a second book. This future book will offer a comprehensive perspective on how a Deaf (or hearing, for all it matters) person can truly work through these issues and truly be happy, in addition to advice in many different areas of life, love, work, etc.

We all are beautiful people, some with fractured minds and broken souls. I still have a sad heart from time to time, my mind still gets confused and conflicted. But the most important thing is: I finally assumed control. I have the control over the biggest and smallest things. I no longer will allow these disorders to control my life.

You can control these problems, those psychological issues that may have plagued you for years. If you feel you have these problems or more, get some help. If you feel you wish to keep it private, by all means, go ahead! Privacy is important to many people, myself included.

Just accept the fact that there are times that it is indeed a greater virtue to ask for help than to deny it. I know this because asking for help was the best thing I've ever done for my mental health. Because of this and the love of my family, I am no longer a victim. I am no longer scared or confused. I am no longer in the dark of the exact natures of my clinical problems.

Most of all, I am no longer a boy interrupted.

THE LAMENTATIONS
OF THE LIBRARIAN

S ighing pensively, the master closed the door of the room behind him as he left.

He had forgotten how hard that period of his life was. The fact that he had survived and flourished was put behind him and forgotten. Fortunately, the master now understood that his source of self-esteem and self-worth came from this room. For when one overcomes something, one comes out of it a stronger and happier person. The master had learned not to trivialize his problems; also, he learned how to give himself credit for having endured such difficult situations. He had never given himself much credit for overcoming the unimaginable obstacles of his life. But now he did.

Exhausted by the long hours of exploring, the master decides to take a nap; this nap would prove to be an unnerving experience for the librarian.

A loud, unearthly explosion, accompanied by a rapid burst of light, shook the ground.

The librarian gasped, as he had been outside walking along the river, pondering about his life. He was having such a nice walk, thinking about how many people had helped him, and he was in such a good mood.

He turned to the direction of the sound and vibrations. He ran frantically to the source, and after taking a glance at the scene in front of him, went into a deep, cold, rippling shock and opened his silent mouth. For a second, no sound came out, and after another deep breath, the sound rang out violently.

"*No!*" the master screamed. His screams reverberated throughout his mind and soul, knowing no bounds, and ripped through the crisp autumn air.

His eyes had just seen the worst nightmare of his entire life: the destruction of his precious library. The library had been set on fire by some unknown force, and it was self-destructing. The fire burnt brightly, overpowering the lights of the stars and the moon. His safe life as he knew it was over; there was no turning back, no way to rebuild. The library was on fire, a hellish scene that he never thought would happen.

The fiery explosion had encapsulated the great library; pages and pages of burning papers drifted above the hot currents of the inferno. The great dome window, with its priceless colored glass, had just shattered, sending a shower of broken dreams to the concrete floor. The smell of burnt paint slowly escaped the building. Red-hot flames licked and jumped out of every window, and the great marble walls became black from the soot, black from the master's evil deeds and destruction toward others outside his sanctuary. The grandfather clock shot out of the door and crashed into the front lawn. Portraits of Joshua flew out of windows, seemingly untouched by the flames, and landed out on the front. They lay on the floor, unable to help the master. Priceless Tiffany lamps, antiques, tapestries, and precious *objets d'art* were also expelled from the library. It was as if the library was disgusted with the possessions inside.

The great light of the Lord also escaped through the great round window. The master saw the ball of light drift away into the skies above. He was gone, no longer there to help the master. The Lord had decided that the master had not truly repented for his sins. Salvation was no longer offered to the master; he had abused the love of God. The great Gothic cross on the top of the dome was set ablaze; on the top of the entrance the figures representing the final judgment of the Christ were also set on fire on both the paradise and the hell sides. Only the Christ himself seemed untouched by the fire, His furious eyes staring down at the master with a look of condemnation. With a look of desperation, the master shivered at his stare with his arms open toward him, sobbing and wailing.

Illuminating the cold, starry skies, the library burned like a great sacrificial lamb, smoke billowing toward the heavens above, as if it were purging the library of its hypocritical beauty, beauty that had been gained at the expense of others, beauty that had no meaning, nor usefulness. The master could not turn his head away from the destruction of his beloved home. The Lord wouldn't allow him to. He must watch the destruction of his soul.

His past evils had come to haunt him, to punish him, for all those times when he had hurt people and pushed them away. For all those times he had used his intelligence and charms for personal gain. For all those times he had hurt those who loved him the most. His friends. His teachers. His colleagues. His family. And especially for those times when he had hurt his own mother, a mother whose actions and words had only represented the love she had for him. It was time for him to pay, and there would be no mercy for him this time. He no longer had a second, third, or a fourth chance. The flames roared, as to announce they were coming to claim the body of the selfish master. A look of horror came across his face, as the master felt something grab hold of him.

A tingling, cold sensation crept its way up the master's body, and he found he could not move his feet or his legs. Soon, he could not move his torso, nor could he move his arms or shoulders; soon his neck froze and his head froze. The only thing he could move were his eyes; the only thing that was warm were his tears, flowing down his beautiful, yet motionless face, a face that had finally understood its sins. The master had been turned into a pillar of salt.

His mouth remained open as he screamed.

The German shepherd who had been sleeping at his feet on the bed jumped off and ran off whimpering. The master suddenly woke up; panting and immediately sobbing, he sat straight up in his bed. He could not stop crying, nor had he ever felt this scared before. Quickly scanning his room, he saw his familiar things: the velvet drapery, the four posts of his bed, the tasseled pillows, the bathrobe hanging at his bathroom door, and a whimpering dog that he had come to know and love, sitting in the corner near his Davenport seat. It was just a dream. But how vivid it was! What detail! What horror!

"Come here, Casey. It's okay. It's over," he said softly to the dog. The dog scuffled along the hardwood floor, as if he were afraid of another terrifying outburst. The master sat there, soaked in sweat, and could not think anymore. The dog jumped back on the bed and snuggled up to him. Patting the dog absentmindedly, the master, with an extremely distraught look on his face, could not think of anything else but one thing: It was time for him to change his ways, ways of dealing with people. The time was now; any delay could cost him his own life and his beautiful world that he had worked so hard on building. He had to make things right with people and himself. He had to go back to the Room of the Mirrors. And look at himself for the first time in his life.

I had never truly looked at myself in a mirror inside that room.

I had never truly taken the words of many people, words that showed how shocked or disappointed they were in my talking or behavior, into consideration. I had never understood my insecurities, my dark desires, nor had I ever truly understood the pain inside me, nor why I kept hurting people. For twenty-seven years I kept that room shut. Shut away from the most important person: myself. Shut away in order to preserve my sanity, my happiness, and my goals. Because I never understood myself fully, I had hurt many people, especially those closest to me. I had, on many occasions, let people inside my library, and after deciding they weren't to my standards, kicked them out in the cold. And eventually, I stopped letting people in.

I never learned how to listen to people and understand that they were only trying to help me. Helping me to be a better person. To be a stronger person. To be a happier person. I never tried to be a happier person, to truly accept myself and rule my library with kindness. I've ruled with terror and subjected many, many people to my anxiety and the need for control; I did this because I never understood how it was to trust someone other than my own dearest family members. I never knew what it was like to know myself; how could I be a good friend if I didn't understand myself?

For twenty-seven years I was lonely. So lonely I didn't even know it. So lonely that I'd attach myself to people on a different kind of level, always wanting to talk to people who were not my peers. I never felt comfortable with my own peers. I have many regrets, and after looking into the bathroom mirror, I saw how much I'd hurt people and myself. How extraordinary that I never took the time to look at my own self, yet spent much time looking at other peoples' selves.

The biggest lamentation I have in my entire life is that I never took the time to understand myself. And an even bigger lamentation I have is that I never learned to trust myself and others.

Because of this, I was a lonely person and never knew what it was like to be loved. I was not someone who was worthy of anybody's love. The cold, hard heart inside me could not handle the warmness that seemed to radiate from people whenever they were around me. I just couldn't let it all in. It was too much, the love from other people. And that's why I shut the library for a long time and built a strong, impenetrable wall around my heart. It was time to try to break that great wall of Jericho and blow my trumpet to let the love break down the wall and flow into the great city, a great city in the Promised Land, and to lead myself and my people, people who had always been there, into the fabled city.

For the first time, the master was going to understand himself in a way he never had before. Thus began the lamentations of Joshua, the librarian.

Apprehensively, the master opened the door to the Room of Mirrors; the creak was so loud that he shivered. He was not ready to look inside, but he must.

Darkness enveloped the room; there were no light switches nor were there any beautiful sources of light. The master put out his arms and tried to find something along the walls. Instead, he felt something brush across his forehead: a cord. His hands went up to it, and he realized it was a light bulb overhead. The pale light flickered on as the master pulled down the cord; it was eerie and cast many shadows in the room's corners. It was the bathroom light, and it also revealed the bathroom mirror, the one that was always used by the master, yet one that he never really looked into. He never understood what was standing in front of him. He never had. He had always refused to look into it longer than he had to.

A worn-out mirror stood on the bathroom wall, it was not pretty, nor was it fancy. It was bleak, grim, and dreary. And it was cold in the bathroom. It was as it was, just a bathroom mirror, and it was not one that lied to you. The master looked around. The room was full of mirrors of various sizes and various styles. The mirrors seemed to have some type of pale, opaque reflections to them; they were the mirrors that made the master feel better about himself. Indeed, they were the mirrors that agreed to deceive him by telling him things he wanted to hear. But not this one.

Grudgingly, the master looked at the run-down mirror and sighed.

"Here I am, standing in front of you, as I should. Show me your true self," the master spoke to the mirror, hoping for a reaction. He did not know what to expect.

The mirror did not respond. It did not speak back. Instead, the master only saw his own reflection. There were no balls of lights, no music, no objects of art, or anything that the master was accustomed to. He began to feel uncomfortable, as he did not feel proud or happy. There was nothing but silence. And his reflection showed an empty, vacant expression, one that indicated the loss of innocence. Slowly, the mood of the master changed. A sense of realization swept across him, a realization that he was missing something. The master began to feel sad and depressed. The sinister mirror was slowly sending thoughts of reality to the master, reality that he cared not to know about.

Quickly, the master attempted to pull the light bulb, but the cord would not turn it off. The master picked up a piece of drywall from the floor and attempted to smash the light bulb. It refused to shatter. Sighing to himself, the master began to turn around and leave. He didn't want to deal with this at all. He wanted out! He didn't like this at all. But something happened.

He could not walk. He could not move. He was stuck to the linoleum floor, his body facing toward the mirror. And an unknown force grasped his chin and forced him to look square into the mirror. Slowly, a greenish light began to emit from the cold surface, and the master could see people moving inside it, people he knew. The scenes played out in front of the eyes of the master; he could do nothing but watch and feel a sense of overwhelming guilt.

"Josh, why did you pull her earring? Do you realize how hurt she could have been?" the principal said to me. He looked gravely concerned. I was in fourth grade, and I had gotten into trouble for pulling a girl's ear; her ear had begun to bleed. I sat there, indifferent, and responded with an attitude.

"She's fine, right? I was just playing. It's over. Done. Why are you making a big deal out of this?" I said.

The principal sighed and muttered something to my teacher, Marla Bales. An expression of grave concern flashed across her face and stayed there. She knew I was developing a serious problem, and something had to be done about it.

Lamentation 1: Every little aggressive behavior I committed caused everybody around me to become concerned. I got in trouble quite often for those physical things during elementary school. And it followed me for a very long time. While my physical aggression had diminished greatly by the time I entered high school, still, the source of my anger was undiscovered. Indeed, this scene was the first of many that showed my disregard for human feelings. I lament over this. The sight on that girl's face had forever burned into my memories. I had really hurt her. I lament over having hurt people just because I was in a dark place.

Looking over my shoulder to check the position of the clerk, I quickly readied myself in front of the merchandise. The Walkman was something I had always wanted for a long time. We didn't have the extra cash at that time, and it was expensive in those days. Still,

I wanted one to impress my friends. And nothing was going to stop me from getting what I wanted.

Taking one final look at the clerk's register and scanning the ceilings for any security cameras, I quickly plucked the Walkman and put it into my coat pocket. I then walked past the clerk, and with my sweetest tone of voice and a pleasant face, greeted her, "Thank you so much. I was just browsing, and I'll be back next week to buy something, okay?"

"Sure, hon. You be careful all right?" she responded with a great smile.

I walked down toward the exit of the store and stepped out into the plaza of the shopping mall, a smug smile on my face. I had scored a free Walkman, and I was "the man." And then I joined my Mommy and my sister, who were out at a different shop.

Lamentation 2: I had shoplifted this one time during grade school. I still think about how I had deceived that sweet lady and stole that Walkman. I wonder if I could ever walk back to Crossroads Mall in Oklahoma City and give them a check for that amount. I had felt so guilty about this crime that I never did it again. While I was generally a very good boy, there were times I behaved otherwise.

"Oh yeah? Well, you tell your father I'm glad he's *six feet under*!" I snapped back at a very close friend of mine in high school. A look of shock came across her face, and she did not respond. The teacher and the sign language interpreter stood there, their mouths open. Nobody could believe I would be so impolite and cruel. I just had brought up her father's recent death as an attack weapon, and it nearly destroyed her. I immediately knew I had done the unspeakable. It would be almost ten years before she would forgive me. To this day, I feel terrible.

Lamentation 3: I brought up the death of someone's father, whom she loved very much, and deliberately used that to hurt her. I had temporarily profited from the situation, and for the longest time, nobody wanted to be around me. I had succeeded in losing many friends that day. No matter how angry or upset one might get, never, ever, ever disrespect those who have passed away.

> The master could not watch any longer; it was becoming a little too much for him. His breathing became shallow and heavy, and he was having a hard time not crying. He was seeing how he had hurt people so much.

"Why did you hit me?" my sister cried. "I didn't do anything!" She continued crying, confused at why her big brother, her protector, would hit her for no reason.

"Because you upset me! You are supposed to do the chores! Oh man, I'm sorry; are you okay? I didn't really mean to. Are you okay?" I said after realizing what I had done. I had slapped my very young sister on the head, and this had happened a few times during my lifetime. I knew it was the wrong thing to do, and to this day, I never have forgiven myself.

Lamentation 4: I hit my little sister. She never deserved it. The amount of guilt I feel cannot be measured nor expressed. I had hit someone that I was designated to protect and nurture. While this has gone behind as time passed, it still dances in my head, even to this day. I know I was not what one would call a child abuser, but still, I feel this way, for I loved and still love my sister, the sweetest girl anybody could ever meet.

> Still, the memories changed from one scene to another. And to the master's horror, the scene began to center around the person he loved the most: his mother.

The television screen shattered. Another object crashed into the wall of the house. Another object was smashed. Mommy and Christina were huddled in the kitchen, terrified.

I was seventeen and having a major emotional melt-down. I was destroying the living room, angry out of my mind, and unable to control my emotions. There was something seriously wrong with me. Never had I felt like this before. I proceeded to the garage, grabbed a weed trimmer, and opened the garage door. A brand-new, glistening Amigo car sat outside on the driveway, unaware of what was to come. Amid screams of horror, I raised the weed trimmer and smashed the windshield of the new car and proceeded to smash it. My screams of rage could be heard across the street. An hour later, sirens wailed, and the police took me to the mental institution for young adults. I had upset my Mommy and Christina so much they didn't want to see me for a good period of time. I had snapped big time. And I stayed in that hospital for a long, long time.

Lamentation 5: The fact I destroyed a brand-new car of Mommy's, which had not yet been insured, still haunts me to this day. While all has been forgiven and forgotten, I could not help but wonder of the severity of my actions. I had snapped, and while I'd been able to get the help I needed, I never came to terms with the nightmare I put my family through. I'm very thankful for counseling, which has helped me identify some major problems, and with that, I was able to quietly ignore myself, provided that I didn't engage in anything like that again. But to ignore and forget things does not mean the problems had disappeared; indeed they had followed me all the way through college and thereafter.

Lamentation 6: I did not learn from my mistakes. And because of this, for a long time, I repeated them over and over. While the degree of severity had dropped, I still had found a way to evolve from physical to verbal in terms of releasing my anger.

The master stood glued to the floor, aghast, and sick to his stomach. He had just seen some of the things that he had tried to forget, things that he had to look at for the first time. The mirror's light died down. It was now just the bare light of the flashbulb.

Suddenly, a sound burst out, startling the librarian.

"You have seen yourself, Joshua. Now, it is time for you to look at the world, the world that you had ignored for so long," the mirror spoke.

The mirror's surface beamed that same green light, and scenes came into sight. What the master saw were those that he had tried to ignore, problems of the world that he didn't want inside his heart; they were too much for him to bear.

The body of a young teenager lies in a car, smashed in; he had been killed by an intoxicated driver.

An AIDS patient lies in a hospital bed. He is dying. His body is skeletal thin and covered in sores. He has no family. His eyes are dry; he cannot cry any more.

A Nicaraguan girl sits on a table, sad and hungry; she is poor and has no parents. She will soon die from starvation and disease.

A tsunami has just wiped an entire village and swept it out to the sea. Images of people crying and heartbroken flashed in front of the librarian.

A scene showing a federal building blown apart in the master's hometown; a firefighter also is carrying the burnt body of an infant. Terrorism had hit close to his heart.

An animal-rights group tries to save the animals after a big oil spill off the coast of Alaska. The animals look miserable in the thick crude oil. And many of them die.

Children of South Africa walk around the slums of their desolate villages outside prosperous cities; they are hungry and have not eaten in days. Their bellies are swollen with worms, and AIDS have claimed their parents.

A homeless man tries to stay warm in the harsh winter in our nation's capital; his frostbitten hands are no longer a concern for him. He needs soup or a warm cup of coffee or else he'll freeze to death.

Polluted rivers spew toxic waste; cancer rates rise sharply in unregulated areas of the world.

A picture shows genocide in Darfur.

An image of a mass grave at a Nazi concentration camp from the Holocaust flashed across the mirror.

And finally, a prolonged scene played out in front of the master: a Deaf young boy at recess being jeered at because of his new hearing aids. There is nothing but hurt and tears on his face. The kids are calling him names, and he is now no longer one of them.

With a scream, the master told the mirror to stop. The mirror complies, and the master is freed from his spot. He ran out of the room, slammed the door, and ran as fast as he could toward the oak ladder, through the trapdoors, until he was outside. He had seen enough. The master had a very hard time breathing. He took a deep breath and tried not to care. He released great, big sobs in between breaths. He couldn't let it in. Not right now. This was not the time.

"Not today, please. It's too much!" the master blurted out, his back to the façade of the library. A hand touched his shoulder ever so gently; the master looks up behind to her.

It was his mother. And she had crept out of her portrait to comfort him after hearing his cries. A look of sadness wore heavily on the woman's face; she knew one day her son would realize everything he had done, and support was what he needed right now. Grabbing her hand and leaning his cheek upon it, the master sniffled and closed his eyes for only a precious moment until he would have to face it all over again. The mother knelt down beside him. She hugged him and patted his back.

Lamentation 7: I mourn for the world and its problems. I lament at the fact that I have ignored them; it was not that I didn't care. I made myself not care, for it was too much. But in doing so, I have blocked my potential to become a leader, a leader who could make a dent in the conflicts of this world. A dent is a difference, and to be a leader, one must learn to accept both the ugly and the beautiful things of life. Too many people adopt the attitude of "Well, I can't do anything about it." But you can.

Lamentation 8: I especially mourn the fact that I did not remain close to my higher power, which is the Lord, during my high school and college years, for he could have helped me form a better sense of myself; I no longer could have done it on my own. I lament over the disappointments I've created for my Father.

Lamentation 9: I also mourn the fact that due to my lack of understanding about myself, I've dissolved many of my friendships into the oceans of anger and sadness. While some of them have stood by me against the test of time and faith, many others have abandoned me.

A final scene played out right in front of the master, but it took him a while to realize it.

For he was looking at himself. He was watching his own reflection, a reflection that represented the exact nature of the master's facial expressions, wrinkles, and what have you. The sad young man in the mirror looked right back at the master with the equally sad, vacant expression. He looked very lost and distraught, and his complexion represented someone who abused his body for earthly pleasures, too much drinking and yielding too much to life's sinful temptations, which had taken its toll on his body. However, a tiny, yet strong glimmer of innocence streaked across the eyes of the person on the other side of the mirror. There was still goodness in Joshua.

But the master didn't see the glimmer. He hated himself too much to even make an attempt to see anything positive. He didn't think he was a good person anymore. For the first time, the master voluntarily abandoned his happy place and stayed outside without any external incentives. Indeed, the master was shocked to see how much he hated himself.

Lamentation 10: I never liked myself because I was Deaf. I always have felt, and do to this day in some ways, like Pinocchio. My ears are wooden, so my language, mind, and soul are full of splintered wood. I never felt I was good enough for anybody. I truly always felt like a broken product, a damaged piece of goods that was to be sent back to the store immediately. I always had felt like a burden on my family. Because I was Deaf. Because I was different. And that had caused me to internalize some very negative things toward the Deaf people, and it was not until I went to Gallaudet that I realized how wonderful Deaf people are, just like their hearing counterparts.

I lament that I have never loved myself, accepted myself, or disclosed myself as a person who can't hear as well as others. I lament at the fact that I never understood that I was truly loved. That people have cried for me. That people have prayed for me. That I have upset people, causing them to become angry with me. And most of all, the eleventh lamentation of Joshua is that I must accept that I will never be perfect. No matter how hard one works, one cannot be perfect. I lament and mourn that I have not recognized my abilities and talents, and because I didn't like myself at all, I never knew how to love others. I have finally faced my worst enemy: me. You are truly your own best friend and your own worst enemy.

The lamentations of the librarian have helped me realize that.

"ARE YOU THERE, GOD? IT'S ME."

Before I can continue with my story, it's important that I take a good look at my relationship with God and how he has been a part of my life for many years.

This may be a boring chapter for a lot of people. Or this might be a very insightful chapter. My beliefs shall not be forced upon you. That is not how we Christians should go about our God. Instead, let me show you how he has helped me keep things in perspective and how his presence has made a huge difference in my life, even in times where I felt lost.

Here is how I have put faith into something I have never seen but felt.

> The master opens the door titled "God and Me," prepared for the usual flash of light that emits from there. However, this time, the light did not burst out; there were neither light nor singing in the background. God had departed for some strange reason, and the master was forced to ponder the reasons why he was not there.
>
> "Are you there, God? It's me, Josh. Where are you, please?" the master called out. His voice echoed throughout the massive library.

No response. He called out again. Still no response.

Puzzled, the master decided to sit down on a chair inside the room and thought about some things.

For many of my friends, this will be the first time they have read or heard me talking about our heavenly Father. While this would certainly surprise and even shock some people who know me well, there is an underlying reason why I had never truly talked about him, why I never disclosed the fact that I was a true Christian, a person whose inner beliefs and convictions revolved around the Savior of my religion. Why I would refuse to impart on others my beliefs.

The reason is simple: I never knew how to talk about Him.

In today's world, the concept of political correctness has, in many ways, made discussion of religion a somewhat uncomfortable subject for conversation among many young people. This is especially true if you were a new college student away from home for the first time, in a big city where politics and shrewdness seemed to mix very well. This would be where starting a new life seemed like the most important thing to you, where a misstep could cost you a great deal in terms of success and advancement; revealing your private beliefs could make you an outsider.

Of course, now I know that's not entirely true. I was very inexperienced in how to successfully integrate myself among people at a very young age and not be so afraid to illustrate to others the goodness in my heart and where it came from. My idea of the world was much different than the actual fact. I was raised in the Bible Belt of America, where going to church was simply a big part of life. Because of the fact I was in a different area of the United States, I wandered off far away from him, into a world where there seemed to be very little spiritual evidence of God. I just wanted to fit in with the new world I found myself in. As time went by, to my surprise, I discovered that more and more people believed in God or some form of a higher power; only then did I feel more comfortable talking about God and his Son.

As someone who has always been interested in good theology, I often come at odds with some verses quoted in the Bible; there have been numerous times when I looked at a verse and scoffed; I couldn't understand the true meaning behind it. With theology comes a better understanding of the Scriptures. And with having guidance in the form of a church or a pastor, better understanding can be achieved.

We are human beings, and we often have a great deal of difficulty trying to make choices, choices that affect our religious beliefs and the types of churches we want to attend. It matters not what your religious beliefs are; we obviously struggle with that from time to time, the choice to accept a specific religion or none at all. It is a difficult thing to do, deciding which faith is the "right" one.

Again, whatever religion anybody chooses is private business. I'm the type of person who accepts everybody. Diversity has always been a big word in my library, and I would not be a good Christian if I rejected anything or anybody different from me.

But for me, God is my first choice. I say this not because I want to be accepted. It's because I feel him and his Son in my heart, a heart that serves as my conscience. Which brings us to the fact that I had not behaved like a good Christian for many years. Only after I truly created my lamentations did I think about my relationship with my Lord and how I could incorporate him into my life without making myself look self-righteous. I was self-righteous in many ways. I wanted to change that. I wanted to be the person everybody could feel comfortable around, someone that one could relate to.

A television set in the room was present, and for some reason the master felt it was important to turn it on.

Flickering images danced across the old television screen, scenes that depicted the great struggle of the Hebrew slaves under the heel of the Pharaoh's brick masters. Scores and scores of exhausted, waiflike shapes struggled as their tired feet trampled the mud underneath; the narrator declared their bondage, how the slavery had been passed from one generation to other. How the tiring task was never ending, how the Hebrews would never know the comforts that their Egyptian counterparts experienced, and how their suffering had formed them together as one blessed, yet cursed people. The master was glued to the screen, staring at the suffering and the dull agony of the chosen people. For some reason, he immediately understood their sufferings and their pain. He understood what it was like to be oppressed, laughed at, and ignored. The master knew what it was like being unable to realize his full potential.

The original movie, *The Ten Commandments*, has for many years remained one of his favorites. Nothing else had ever so brilliantly depicted the endurance of the human spirit and how the belief in something could help it endure the suffering and pain that it had gone through. Nowhere else in the history of cinema had there ever been a film that took such a serious insight to the sacred Scriptures of the Holy Bible and successfully transported that to the silver screen. This movie helped the master understand God more.

Because of this, in addition to having been in church since the age of five, God has become the master's guidance; the everlasting burning bush had become his motif, a motif representing hope and faith, a motif that showed how God would never run out of love and guidance. The fire on that bush still burns on for many of his followers.

As a Deaf man whose world is heavily dependent on visual imagery, the powerful scenes depicting the parting of the Red Sea and Moses' conversation with God on Mount Sinai enabled the master to envision what it would be like to talk to the Lord. Despite the fact that the master has a very imaginative mind, he does like to envision the scene of the burning bush and how the Lord's presence should not be taken lightly. For the master, God still has yet to part the Red Sea. The sea has not been parted, for the time to be a leader has not yet been revealed. The master is not yet ready. Only time will tell, and when the time is ready, he will speak to the master's heart.

When the master is ready, he will know it fully, without any doubts, and he will take on the task left to him by Moses, one that gave him the responsibility of leading the people into the Promised Land. Only then will the reason for all the struggles and pain will be revealed. Only then will the master see his true purpose in life. Now is not the time. The master sighed and turned off the television. He sat in the room, wondering where his God was. He was nowhere in that room.

What happened? Where did he go?

Then Samuel took the horn of oil, and anointed him in the midst of his brethren: and the Spirit of the Lord came upon David from that day forward. So Samuel rose up, and went to Ramah.

1 Samuel 16:13 (KJV)

Now I know that the Lord saveth his anointed; he will hear him from his holy heaven with the saving strength of his right hand.

Psalms 20:6 (KJV)

The sacrifice of the wicked is an abomination to the Lord: but the prayer of the upright is his delight.

Proverbs 15:8 (KJV)

This is my insight as a Christian as to what these verses above mean. They talk about being anointed with oil, how you will come into the Lord's good favor, and how prayers are powerful.

The first two verses are perhaps very important for two possible reasons.

The first reason is if you are a newborn child or a very young one, in terms of spirituality, you could benefit from these verses if your family is of Christian faith. We all know that at one point in our lives, after passing the stage of innocence as children, we must decide whether or not to accept Jesus Christ the Savior as a part of our daily lives. I've learned that all young children go to heaven, no matter how terrible they had been. All children that have not yet been able to understand evil are protected. I may be opening up an issue for debate in the Christian network, but I also believe that if one is also anointed at infancy (for the right reasons, only when the entire family has the best intentions at heart), he will be further protected until the time he can determine whether or not he wants Christ in his life. The second reason is if you are pondering God as a part of your life, at least seriously, then the best way to begin is to anoint yourself with prayers, so you can enter the preparations of how you can begin to accept him as a big part of your life and to best serve him.

The first verse discusses King David and how he was able to have the good grace of the Lord after being anointed with oil. The second verse talks about how if you are anointed (this can mean either being anointed literally or accepting God as a part of your life), you are enabled with the strength of the Lord.

The thing about these first two verses that strikes a chord in my heart is that I've seen my life as an example of how protected I was. Since I was a newborn, a series of accidents and illnesses had seemed to break and hurt my body, but still, with the anointed oil that my grandfather had bestowed upon my forehead at fifteen months, I seemed to pull through, surviving these situations. Of course, people could argue that there is very little evidence that being anointed with oil (literally, as I was by my grandfather, who was a minister in his days) would ensure your safety. This is a matter of spirituality and faith.

But I can't help but notice that for all the things I've been through, I still came out of them with an intact soul and mind. I've been injured more than a young boy should. I've been torn and ripped apart, only to recover quickly. In terms of cruel insults, I've been called a potential statistic and someone who would not accomplish much in life because of my Deafness. But, for me, I believe that the anointed oil sealed a sheet of protection over my body and my heart, thus enabling me to continue on the very uncertain path that I've been on for years now.

Perhaps the metaphor "being anointed with oil" simply illustrates to the prayers and the faith my family had put into my future. This brings us to the third verse, which discusses the power of faith-filled prayers. I think if you pray, you have to mean it. You can't pray in vain if you don't really have God in your heart and if you pray for selfish purposes.

The prayers and the faith of my grandmother, Mommy, father, and many others seemed to have placed upon me ensured that my earthen vessel would be protected in order to realize its full potential. So, being anointed through literal application of oil or prayers helps ensure that you are preparing yourself for the greatest life intended for you under the guidance of the Lord.

That is what those verses mean to me, a person who has understood the impact of pain and suffering in his life.

"For God so loved the world, that he gave his only begotten Son, that whosoever believeth in him should not perish, but have everlasting life" (John 3:16, KJV).

It is a simple verse, yet one that has the most profound message from all the books, chapters, and verses of the Bible. This is perhaps the most well-known verse of them all. And it should be. This shows the ultimate act of love and forgiveness known to mankind. And that a gift had been bestowed upon us, the people in the universe, a gift that would ensure that our spiritual well-beings would continue in happiness and peace after our bodies had ceased to exist.

Until today, I have not talked about this in the past eight years. Until today, I've not once talked about how Christ died for me on the cross, at least to others outside my immediate family, simply because I felt it sounded too literal, too blunt, too straightforward, and sometimes a little scary. It's a very bold statement, declaring that I believe that Jesus died on the cross for me, that I've placed an enormous amount of belief and faith into someone who had been hotly debated for centuries. An event that, according to several scholars, never took place, that Christianity is one big lie, that God doesn't exist, that there was no possibility that a Son of his could have existed, that it simply violated the laws of physics and science.

Dear scientists and scholars, you all make an excellent point. I admire your intelligence and educational backgrounds. You all have toiled and earned your PhDs in your own respective fields. I would not want to put you down or speak ill of you. I understand how science and religion could have a conflict. I know because I experience this same type of conflict within. How can I sit here and write that I love the Son of my Lord without even having seen evidence? Without having seen those miracles having been performed? How can I say this, being the librarian, one that loves proof, credibility, and consistency?

I have two answers for you: the Bible and my heart. God's greatest weapon of love is his ability to enter your heart (through the Holy Spirit, as we Christians call it) through the Scriptures in the Bible. God speaks to us from the Bible. We have the Holy Spirit, which acts as our conscience and gives us the ability to understand God's Word. But the best evidence that I can think of, after all these years in church and reading the Bible, is the fact that I felt so terrible before I was ready to ask Jesus to be a part of my life. And how, after asking him to come into my life (being saved), I immediately felt better. That's why I love Him. He is out of reach, physically, but he's right here in my heart.

> Next to the television set the master saw a table with countless Bibles that had been given to him over his lifetime; he also saw stacks and stacks of notes that showed a young man trying to under-stand the book of God and Jesus. There also were various books discussing different faiths, and he also sees some applications to Christian colleges. Books and books specializing in Christian theology stood alone at one corner of the table; they were those that the master had indulged in. An intellectual at heart, he always struggled to pair his mind and his heart when it came to God and religion. Next, he saw some letters and postcards from the pastors that he had known over his lifetime. He saw a picture of a pastor and his wife; those two people were the greatest influence on his religious life. He smiled, for he has nothing but great things to say about these two people.
>
> Joni and Danny Bice had always been the husband and wife who had offered teachings of the Lord in a non-affronting way; they also were

responsible for the guidance of many Deaf people in the area of Oklahoma City, Oklahoma. They were especially important in the small town of Moore, where they still lead the Deaf ministries at First Baptist Church of Moore.

For many years, the master attended the Sunday services and the Bible studies. The church was a new one, a bigger one than his previous church (Southwest Baptist Church of Oklahoma City, under Sunday school teachers Holly Dougharty and Judy Nard). He especially liked the fact that there was a church where all the Deaf people congregated and conducted their own worship services without language barriers. Prayers and songs were done in sign language, and Danny Bice had a wonderful way of deciphering the mysterious, complex messages of the Bible.

It wasn't until the master was older that he finally appreciated all those years of their spiritual leadership, after he was done with college. It wasn't until then that the master realized the profound influence these two people had on his understanding of God and his Son. He just had learned how to appreciate them, especially after seeing that they were two of the most sincere Christians in this world today. This church was also where the master was baptized, a symbol of being born again. It may not seem like a significant event to some people, but for him, being able to proclaim his faith via baptism in front of many, many people with sincerity has forever sealed his love for Jesus Christ, our Savior.

What's more is that these two people may be hearing, but they had incorporated into them the knowledge of the Deaf culture, and they had succeeded in understanding the unique nature of the

Deaf mind, thus enabling themselves to minister God's Word to the Deaf community.

We the Deaf people of Moore, Oklahoma are fortunate to have them as our local spiritual leaders. With their invaluable insight to the Bible and their good, strong hearts, we have been able to call First Baptist Church of Moore our place of worship.

From time to time, whenever I visit Oklahoma, I feel an urge to return to the church and rejoice in the love of our Lord.

> For as he thinketh in his heart, so is he: Eat and drink, saith he to thee: but his heart is not with thee.
>
> Proverbs 23:7 (KJV)

This is one of many verses in the Bible that discusses health and well-being.

It all works together, your body, soul, and spirit. This verse is very important to me because it shows how (after careful analysis and further study, of course) God gives you the ability to fight off anything that might pull down your spiritual health, thus potentially affecting your physical health. It's also important to me because it also reminds me not to abuse my body or cause this vessel of earth to be subject to conditions that could damage it. It reminds me that this body was given to me, and it is my ultimate responsibility to take care of it. God is not going to do everything for me.

It's like what God said: "And be not drunk with

wine, wherein is excess; but be filled with the Spirit" (Ephesians 5:31, KJV).

That's what free will is all about. You control your body, but God is there to guide you. You just have to know how to listen and see the signs of what you are to do with your body. Take the necessary steps to ensure your body is well balanced. Get some help, if necessary, be it medical or spiritually. I've abused my body before, especially during my college years, and am thankful I've found a newfound respect for my own body. Remember always to care for your body, after caring for your soul. It's very easy to forget, especially when you're very young, to take care of yourself.

Health is important, isn't it? With a healthy mind, body, and spirit, you can do anything you want to do. Anything.

> The master became restless and still searched for the Lord in the room. Where was he?
> He was oblivious to the fact that even though the Lord's presence is not seen, it can be felt and recognized in the signs that are all over the room: the television channels, the books, the Bibles, the letters, and the postcards, signatures of a greater being have been left behind.
> Turning back on the television and sitting on the chair once again, the master sighed and crossed his arms. While flipping through the channels of the Christian network with the remote control, he saw a couple of Christian ministers: the funny, down-to-earth Joyce Meyer and Gregory Dickow. He also saw some programs depicting the Catholic Sunday Masses and saw some specials on the condition of the state of Israel.
> Suddenly, something familiar caught his eye:

an extremely positive and appealing speaker smiling and speaking to the audience. The master stopped the flipping and watched the man. Closed-captioning words appeared at the bottom of the television screen. A message that seemed especially suited for the master at that very moment, was typed as the speaker continued with his message.

The person he was watching was, in the master's opinion, the most appealing Christian pastor that he had ever seen before on television; something about the speaker evoked the positive feelings that he had always wanted to feel. Something about him made the master think about how he could change the little things in his life. There was just something about him; he seemed so real, honest, and sincere. And kind. The master almost never bothered with Christian television, but since this kind man had appeared on the network, he always looked forward to his services.

His name was Joel Osteen, and he was the strongest, most positive Christian force on television that had come all the way from Houston, Texas into the library of the master.

Now, there's just something about that pastor from Houston. I don't know what it is about Osteen that appeals to me. Perhaps it's the way he speaks. Perhaps it's the way he smiles. Perhaps it's the way he presents himself. There's that certain *je ne sais quoi* about Osteen. He carries the message of God in a very uplifting, positive way. And I believe that, for many of us, that type of positivism is a much-needed infusion of fresh air in our lives, especially those of us who want to become closer to God. We Christians are tired and worn out from the red-faced evangelists telling all of us that we'd go to hell if we sinned ever again. We are tired of preachers that may not seem honest. We are tired of scandals surrounding seemingly great Christian leaders. We are tired of being concerned on whether or not a pastor's actions are genuine. We are tired of complicated messages. We want something simple, something refreshing.

The most memorable message I remember coming from the Compaq Center in Houston is the one where you don't listen to negativity and rid that from your lives. Osteen preached that the negative comments directed toward you should be bounced back off you because you're anointed by God and that you should never lose your focus on what God has intended for you to do. Don't get dragged down by people's negativity. That was a very big, important message for me. God knows I've had many negative comments thrown at me by people who thought I'd amount to very little. And I've ignored those people for over twenty years. Lately, I've let people get to me, and I'm doing a reversal where I can remain focused and not lose sight of my goals.

I look at this preacher, and he is the epitome of what he preaches: uplifting, positive, sincere, humble, and human. Most of all, he represents what a pastor should be: nonjudgmental.

As successful as he is, Osteen still finds the time to care and stay focused on what he does best: preaching and writing inspirational books that are designed to help improve a person's thinking and perception of life. Most of all, Osteen has been the direct impact on the revitalizing of relationship between me and God. With his strong guiding light in the darkness, he helped me find God again. He helped me look at God at a different angle. God is not angry. He is loving and forgiving. You are given chances throughout your life by Him to do great in your life. By just looking at him, his television ministries have shown me that it is really possible to be the happiest person on this face of earth and not have to abandon God. To know God is to be happy.

There are just so many things I'd love to get into about God and Jesus. But there is always time, a lifetime, to understand him and his Son. We cannot understand him in one chapter. I don't understand him fully, but I'm okay with that. I've got my faith and my health. That's all I need right now to move ahead in life. I've often asked this question, "Are you there, God? It's me." And often, I don't get a response where I'd feel something in my heart. I often get a response from God months later, if not years later, through signs; you'd be amazed at how the Lord works things out for you, if you learn how to read the signs out there. He will never leave you, no matter how lost you might feel.

With that in mind, I'd like to close this chapter with a prayer.

It is only appropriate that I end a chapter about God with a prayer. How could I sit here and tell you I'm a Christian without sending a blessing to the reader, namely, you? You don't have to be a Christian to receive this prayer. Feel free to skip this part and go onto chapter 8 if you are uncomfortable with this.

I wish to bless you, briefly, if that's all right.

Dear Heavenly Father,

Please bless the reader, the one that has been reading this story all along, with the knowledge and wisdom to do well in his or her life; bless the reader with the love that you possess and grant him or her the understanding that everything has a way of working itself out.

Also, I pray that you please bless the families and friends of the reader and that you please watch over them and ensure they all are happy and healthy, that they also make the right choices in their life, be it with or without You.

I ask that you please, no matter what faith the reader might have, bless him or her.

Thank you.

In Jesus' name I pray,

Amen.

(Prayer typed on November 20, 2007, at 11:47 p.m., Eastern Standard Time.)

THE STABILIZING
FACTOR: MY STEPDAD

He had wanted to save this room for one of the last few stops; so important was his stepdad that he wanted to have the luxury of time while reviewing the room of someone who had forever changed his life for better. The master, after having done the usual back-and-forth routine with that old oak ladder, finally arrived to the floor of his dad. A click, turn, and a push of the door later, the master found himself inside the room of the greatest male influence in his life.

Tons of items representing Dad's service in the air force lined up a wall; those were the relics of what he considered the greatest thing, to be a service to his country. In addition to the military memorabilia, there were samurai swords adoring another wall, complemented by uniforms and lesson books in tae kwon do, the art of karate. Also, there were, at a table by the third wall, books and notes pertaining to the human anatomy and nursing; Dad, along with Mommy, had recently become a registered nurse.

Neat, organized, and simple, Dad's room gave a sense of function and simplicity to the visitor.

That order and function also was introduced into the lives of the master and his family.

Change occurs in everybody's life, whether we want it to or not.

A big change occurred to me during my first year at Gallaudet University. I didn't accept the change with the biggest heart or the best attitude. Changes have a way of humbling us, especially when we had formed wrongful impressions of people that enter our lives.

Kenneth was someone I misjudged, and even when Mommy married him, I still bore a resistance to his sudden entry into my life. I sincerely thought he would harm Mommy and leave her high and dry. My annoying Oedipus complex went into complete defense mode. I thought he was someone who would step in and destroy all the good things I had with Mommy. I felt extremely threatened by his presence, yet I decided to put on a pleasant appearance and only spoke to him when the situation warranted it. I thought he would try to hurt me deliberately because he was a stranger.

I'm glad I was wrong.

Call him Ken. Call him the guy my Mommy married. Call him the stepdad. Call him whatever you may. It doesn't matter. To me, he's simply my dad.

Dad, this chapter is dedicated to you.

Sparkling rhinestones adorned the top of the wedding dress. Soft, delicate sheets of chiffon type and satin fabric made up the dress. The dress billowed out from the waist; she looked like a princess about to meet her

Prince Charming. The beautiful auburn hair extensions were securely attached to the woman's head. A simple, elegant veil sat on the top of her perfectly done hair, its train draping from there all the way to the backside. Shimmering diamond earrings hung from her earlobes. Her makeup was picture perfect. This was a portrait of a woman was about to get married to the man of her dreams; indeed, the young bride looked jittery and excited.

She loved the man very much. She never thought she'd find personal happiness in her life again. That day was the first time I had ever seen Mommy so happy. And it was the last time I would ever have her to myself.

"Do you, Diana, take this man to be your lawfully wed husband, to hold in sickness and health, for richer or poorer, for better or worse, and until death shall do you part?" the minister asked my mother after Dad recited his vows to her.

It was May 2, 1998, and I was sitting in the front pew at the small chapel in Oklahoma City, Oklahoma. I had just given my Mommy away at the altar as a part of the ceremony. I almost didn't even fly to Oklahoma for the wedding; I had wanted to spite Mommy. Only after Grandmother called me and told me to get on a plane and have the respect for my mother did I come.

With a painful twinge of silent jealousy, I sat in the front of the church pew, listening to the exchange of the vows. It was all happening so fast. With a polite posture and a pleasant smile on my face, I looked like a son who was very excited for his mother. I blended into the congregation; to the outside world, I was just as happy as everybody.

But inside me, it was a different story. Indeed, it took every grain of my strength to contain the screaming and stomping of the little Deaf boy who was so accustomed to the special attention from his Mommy. I wanted to ruin the wedding and tell everybody it was one big mistake. I sincerely wanted to break it all up. I didn't want this to happen. I was so ready to run to the altar and cause a dramatic scene. I wanted the attention back to where it was supposed to be: me. It was one of the most difficult things I ever had to do, letting my Mommy go.

As the newlyweds turned around to face the audience after the ceremony, I avoided looking at them directly. I didn't want Mommy to see the telltale signs of anger in my eyes and my tense mouth. I didn't want to ruin this day for her. I had to fake everything that day.

"And I present to you the new couple: Diana and Kenneth Cassell," the minister said with a smile after Mommy and Dad had kissed. The couple looked at the audience with happy smiles. As they smiled, the smile I gave in return only concealed the painful realization that I just lost my Mommy in a matter of minutes. The lifetime of a special relationship had just been destroyed within less time than it took to get ready for school.

That day, I thought I was abandoned and left to fend for myself. Of course, I now know that couldn't have been further from the truth; my family life only got better after that day.

Dad and I never were ones to go into flowery prose on things in life; we just have that simplicity that comes with an adult relationship. We just keep things simple. I think that's true for many dads and sons, or at least I imagine it to be so. With Dad, I like how things are not always spoken and discussed; it seems that we understand each other on a different level. We can be in the same room for hours and not say a word to each other; normally that would make me uncomfortable, but it's never been that case with Dad.

Because of this, I will get right to the point here. I will just list the major things I've learned from him during the past ten years in which he had been a father to me. So, here's why you're important to me, Dad. Let me list five major reasons why you've become a father to me.

Reason 1: Dad changed the way things worked in the family.

How many of you out there have a stepparent? And an even more important question is: how did you feel when they entered your life unexpectedly? Was it a welcome change or was it a change that caused a great deal of apprehensiveness within you? It took me about five years before I began to recognize him as a father figure; it took me so long because I had seen Mommy get married before, only to see the marriage dissolve and witness the negative impact it had on her. Naturally, I had to watch and wait before I'd even consider extending my affection toward him.

He changed many things in the family for better after the wedding. The first thing that I noticed was how Mommy was less anxious and more secure with herself. And she was a lot happier, and I was not accustomed to that. Indeed, as time passed, Mommy began to become more independent and less worried about assuaging my anxiety or worries. She still cared about me, naturally, but she made it clear that her new husband came first. And suddenly, I was put in the "real world," where I had to understand and accept the fact that Christina and I were no longer in front of the line.

Dad changed all that. Gone were the days of manipulation. Gone were the days of excessive attention. Gone were the days of *moi, moi, moi*. Gone were the days of flagrant disregard for Mommy's feelings.

There came the days of more respect. Came the days of realism. Came the days of order and structure. Came the days of financial security. And most of all, there came finally a father figure, one that I had been in desperate need of.

He made Mommy happy, and he completed the family unit, forever stabilizing the portraits inside my library. I had finally accepted him as the ultimate authority figure, and that was a change I was willing to accept after many years. In addition to this, I finally understood the idea of tough love. Too many children seem to be selfish and spoiled these days. Too many parents seem to give in to their children's demands. And that always creates a tension and friction within a household. He changed the way I saw how things should work within a family.

Reason 2: Dad unknowingly helped me understand the concept of how to be a strong, dependable young man.

In the past ten years, I've become a lot happier and more comfortable in my own skin. The reason is simple: I learned what being a strong young man was about.

In a world where a dominant male was absent, I've

been given the great opportunity to explore the world of feelings, words, affection, and the softer nuances of life. I thank my family, which had an overwhelming majority of strong women, for the rare chance of experiencing that. However, the introduction of Dad into my life gave me a firsthand experience on what a strong, responsible man was all about. It gave me an opportunity to explore a different side of me, one that I never gave much thought to. That side in which I had been able to explore showed how capable I was of being responsible, not only for myself, but for others around me: family, friends, and colleagues.

And that being responsible is really a simple thing, one that isn't laden with the complexities of feelings or emotions; Dad taught me that one should learn how to remove his emotions outside any type of situation in order to make some command decisions in the best way possible. For too long I've allowed my emotions to grasp control of my logical functions; I've often let them interfere with my ability to make well thought-out plans. With responsibility comes self-control. How can you be responsible without knowing the importance of self-control, particularly when it comes to handling situations with propriety? Again, Dad helped me further examine that.

For the longest time, I've lacked the basic ability to maintain self-control over my thoughts and what came out of my mouth. I'd scream or say things that I later would regret; because of Dad (and of course, everybody else in the family and some professors at college), I've finally realized that it is indeed a virtue to remain silent rather than to be abrasive to the point where it would do a lot more harm than good.

In addition to having finally come in touch with my

masculine side, I have, over the past few years, become a stronger person in every way possible. It's really as simple as that. And Dad is important to me in the sense that he helped me realize that, maybe after all, I'm a simple person. Maybe I wasn't as complicated as I thought I was. Maybe if I took the time to remove all the stressful things, I could see how I also wanted a life that was much simpler.

Reason 3: Dad accepted my Deafness without any hesitation.

You know, I've heard many stories where parents or stepparents had a very hard time accepting their children because of their Deafness (or any other disabilities). They were embarrassed by the differences between them and their children. They didn't want society to mock them, to look at them as strange or different.

Dad didn't care about that. He was never one to focus on trivial issues like that. Indeed, from day one, he had never mentioned or showed that my Deafness was an issue for him. That was an extremely significant thing, to be accepted by someone that had been brought into the family, no questions asked. To be accepted for who I was, not what I was. Dad accepted me. He embraced who I was and didn't try to make me feel inferior because of my so-called disability. He impressed me with his ability to look beyond that and look at me as a person, a person he wanted to include in his new life.

And because of that, it was even easier for me to accept him as a father to me.

Reason 4: Dad showed me the value of being frugal and how saving money could take you very far in life.

As I had already mentioned in the chapter about

Mommy, wise financial management had never been my strength. Indeed, I'd spend every dollar I earned or received on ridiculous things that didn't last for very long. It was not something I saw as a tool, the idea of money. I saw it as a ticket to short-term happiness and instant gratification. I had always been able to get pretty much what I needed, a little bit of money here and there whenever I needed it. I had always been able to talk Mommy into giving me that twenty-dollar bill so I could run to Starbucks or some fast food place.

Dad changed that. It was as if a big wet towel was slapped across my face. For the first time, I was constantly given the word I hated the most: no.

Conversations would take place quite often during the early years of the marriage between Mommy and Dad:

"Dad, can I have ten dollars?"

"No."

"Mom?"

"Sorry, honey. He says no."

"Dad, can I borrow one hundred dollars for a plane ticket and I'll pay you back next month?"

"No."

"Dad, please?"

"No."

And I'd throw a fit and say how cheap he was and how he was trying to make me suffer. And then a big argument would erupt among Mommy, Dad, and me. Naturally, I now know that isn't true. As time went by, I started to understand how things worked in terms of finances and budgeting.

Wasn't that sad, to see that I was almost into my thirties with a college degree and didn't even know how to manage a monthly budget?

He wanted me to learn, to *really* learn how to take care of myself; taking care of myself financially would always mean that I'd never find myself in a situation where I'd have to ask for a loan, where I'd never have to present to my parents any type of financial concerns, where I'd just simply take care of myself, as each young man or lady should. Dad also didn't believe in conspicuous consumption; we all never were ones to purchase extravagant gifts or over-the-top things, as debt was the last thing he wanted in our lives. Frugality and living by necessities are only some of the biggest improvements in my personal life, and it's all because of him.

Thank you, Dad. Thanks for being tough on me.

Reason 5: The final reason is simple: Dad made Mommy happy.

There you have it.

I have to admit one thing. I was always worried about Mommy, worried about if she would be all right by herself when I went off to college. It did my heart good that she at least, if temporarily, had someone right before I left for college. It also made me happy knowing that Mommy was happier, not only as a mother, but also as a woman. Once I had seen, after a few years, how serious Dad was about Mommy, I began to understand that it was possible for her to be happy, and it had helped me move on with my own life, knowing Mommy was just fine with Dad. And for the first time, I saw it was possible for *me* to be happy in my own life.

Because Dad made Mommy happy, I was able to slowly let her go and not feel so dependent on her (emotionally and mentally) as I pursued the things I wanted in my own life.

I've listed the reasons. I've described them to you

briefly. But I yet still have to talk about the personal side of Dad. My favorite thing about him is that he has the oddest sense of humor, humor that is not typically found anywhere. And he always brought an element of unpredictability in our family vacations, with his innate nature as a practical joker. A particular scene comes to my mind where I fell victim to one of his antics.

The rushing, foamy waters of the James River proved its cold, icy presence. Streaming and meandering through the forestry hills of Virginia, the mighty river declared its power and its ability to swallow up anything that dared to fall in it.

Putting sunscreen on my skin and shielding my eyes from the noon sun, I sat in a canoe with Dad while a separate canoe held Mommy and Christina. We had taken upon ourselves the task of taking a day away from our home in Richmond and decided to venture out into the wilderness and enjoy ourselves on this fine summer day. Conversations were exchanged along the way downstream; everybody was in a great mood, including me. It was so nice to have been able to take some time off from my temporary job and spend the day with my family.

Little did I know I'd be completely soaked from head to toe.

"Hey, Josh. That's a nice hat you got," Christina said to me. She and Mommy had begun to row closer to our canoe. "Can I see it?" she continued.

"Oh, thanks! Sure, here," I said with a smile as I handed my baseball cap over to her extended hand.

"Hey, can you stand up real quick?" she said with a convincing smile.

For some reason, I had not noticed anything strange about this request. Dad was whispering something to Mommy, and she was giggling.

Impervious to what was going on around me, I stood up on the canoe; I was right in front of Dad.

With a smile and a gleeful tone of voice, I declared, "What a nice day! Don't you think, Christina? Is there something in the water? What am I looking for?"

Christina and Mommy sat in their canoe with suppressed, stiff smiles.

Suddenly, without any warning, the canoe rocked. Completely taken aback, I gasped as my feet struggled to maintain contact with the rubbery surface of the interior; Dad had caused the canoe to sway back and forth sideways. With a scream, I toppled off the canoe and plunged headfirst into the icy, cold water. The cold encapsulated my entire body, and I felt the immediate reaction of being submerged in forty-degree water— shivering and chattering my teeth. Laughing and stomping his feet, Dad looked at me and doubled over. He kept saying, "I love ya, man. I had to do that!"

Shocked and freezing, I told him to let me swim along the current and try to get to the closest riverbank. I laughed, partly out of shock and anger, as I swam closer and closer to the bank. That was my favorite memory of a vacation with Dad. He had expertly dumped me into a river, and I didn't have a problem with it. Naturally, I was a lot more cautious from that day on. Dad would continue to surprise me with his arsenal of jokes and pranks.

But seriously, I'm not sure how I can complete this

chapter. It was one of the more difficult chapters to write.

It is not because it's hard to write about him; it's just that I have not yet found the words, in my opinion, which could appropriately describe him.

Such a task this has been, that I have decided that a nice, simple chapter would be the best way to describe Dad, for he is simple, logical, and truly one of a kind. He is the best thing that has ever happened to this family.

Thank you, Dad.

Thank you for accepting me as a son of your own. I'm proud to call you my dad.

Love,

Josh

AUNT JULIE: AUNT, FRIEND, AND MENTOR

Closing his stepfather's door behind him, the master thought about how important the people in his life were.

Unlike many people in the world, the master took the time to recognize the contributions of the countless people in his life. He recognized that credit must be given to many people; without them, the master would have not been where he was. Indeed, there was one more person inside the library that the master wanted to recognize: his aunt.

Carrying the thought inside him, the librarian knew he would have to climb to the highest levels of the library to enter the room of his favorite aunt. Directly beneath the last door, which was locked with that familiar heavy padlock, lay the floor holding the room of Aunt Julie. The master arrived to this door out of breath and opened it with the antique key.

Inside the room there were contemporary furnishings, and everywhere there contained countless objects that represented serenity of the Floridian lifestyle: seashells, beach pebbles, sand fossils, nautical décor, and furnishings that were contemporary with accents representing the nuances of the great African safari landscape. Inside the room also stood various pots of palm trees, a swimming pool, and a spacious porch. It was like entering a beach house: airy, shabby yet chic, and simple. It was also peaceful and organized. The master loved being around his favorite aunt, for she always had an inspirational feel to her.

Suddenly, a voice rang out from the porch. He could see a young woman moving into view. She sported an athletic body and red hair; she was also dressed in the casual attire, with bright colors, which was ever so typical of a Floridian resident.

"Hey, Josher! What's up?" the young aunt's voice tickled the master's hearing aid.

The master looked to the direction of the voice and laughed. He then walked over to Aunt Julie's side and greeted her.

"I'm great, thanks!" he responded.

"Want to go out for lunch?" Aunt Julie said with a great big smile.

"That'd be fabulous! I'm starving," said the librarian.

"Good! Let's go. We'll take my car. Let's go to the beachside and have something to eat," Julie said as they walked toward the door.

I like to believe that for each of us there is that one special person in the family that seems to be more of a buddy than a family member. In my opinion, it's very important to have a friend within the family that would offer you a different angle on things in life. Certainly, Mommy is my first and favorite, but it's always nice to have someone else in the family that you can be friends with.

She is a family member whom you could talk to

about anything, without the fear of being chastened or scolded at. She was also a member that, for some reason, I became glued to during my young childhood years.

And most of all, someone that could offer advice and feedback in almost every area of your life: school, education, dating, and conflict resolution of relationships with family members. Besides Grandma and Mommy, Julie has been there for me for as long as I could remember. She is not only my favorite aunt. She is also a friend and a mentor to me.

No question about it.

Julie is not just someone I say hello to every once in a while. She has, over the past twelve years, become someone that I could relate to. Our similarities lie in how we perceive life and how we like to go about things.

There are many things that have further strengthened our very unique friendship, a friendship that every child would aspire to have with his aunt or uncle. And food was always central to our social visits.

Here's why.

Summer 1981

The young high school graduate sat at the breakfast table, with a bag of McDonald's fast food; she sat next to a young toddler, seated in a high chair. She proceeded to pull out the food from the bag and began to eat. The toddler quickly recognized the food, and located his desired gastronomical pleasure: McDonald's French fries. While the girl was looking away from her food, the toddler reached over his high chair table and expertly grabbed the French Fries, one by one, until the girl noticed the crime.

Scoffing, the girl tried to hide her bag of food, including the fries. The boy was annoying her, and she wanted to eat alone in peace. The boy wanted the fries and wouldn't give up. He began to whine and wail, slowly going into a mini temper tantrum.

"Diana! Josh keeps eating my fries!" Aunt Julie said in indignation. I was eyeing her McDonald's fries with an obsessive look, and my hands kept reaching for the fry bag.

"I know. He has a thing for French Fries. Just give him some," Mommy said with an unimpressed tone of voice while looking over her shoulder. She was talking to someone on the telephone, and we were in the kitchen of Grandma's.

It was summer 1981, and Aunt Julie was trying to conceal the fries so I wouldn't scream hysterically until she gave me some. I had this obsessive fixture on those fattening sticks of carbs and fat. I still do to this day. The boy began to scream and babble incoherently, as a Deaf toddler would. His screams were beginning to get to Julie. His arms kept extending across the high chair table, and his hands were stretched outwards her.

"Oh, whatever. I give up. Here, Josh. Just take some. Here. Take it," Julie said with a resigned sigh. My grubby hands grabbed and squished the delicate fries; I then stuffed them in my mouth. I then looked at Julie with a curious expression, as if I was trying to locate the hidden bag. I wanted more. Looking at me with a slightly aghast expression, Julie wore an air about her that illustrated a person trying to figure me out; I was her first nephew, and she was fascinated by my unique attachment to her and her food. It was all new to her, having a nephew.

Thus began our tradition of having lunches together; surely, the tradition didn't start until I was in my high school years, but I always joke to myself that the day I stole her French fries was the day that we shared our first lunch together. The most memorable lunch I had with Julie during my high school years took place in the great city of San Antonio, Texas.

It was also the day I learned how to properly pronounce the word of my favorite bread.

San Antonio, Texas. March 1997

This was before I had my nervous breakdown; this was during my senior year in high school. The family and I had gone down to San Antonio to watch Christina compete in the national cheerleading championships (which had placed Christina's cheer team in third place for juniors division). Julie and Robert had flown into the city, whereas Mommy and I rode along with the cheer team on the chartered bus. During a break in the competition, Julie took me out to lunch because I needed some space from the family, being an emotional teenager and all.

"I beg your pardon?" the waiter said

We were at a casual café that had a Mexican feel to it.

The waiter looked at me with a funny expression; I had just ordered some breakfast, and unbeknownst to me, I had mispronounced a specific food item.

"Oh. I said I wanted a *cross-tant,*" I repeated.

"A what?" the waiter looked at me with squinted eyes, a rude expression on his face.

Sighing, I looked to Aunt Julie for some help. Acknowledging the fact that I was embarrassed and frustrated, Julie kindly jumped in.

"Josh," she said gently. "It's not pronounced *cross-tant*. It's *kruh-sahnt*," she continued.

"Oh. Oh! *Kruuu-sahnt?*" I repeated while looking at her lips as I struggled to catch on the proper phonological aspects of the word.

"Yes, close enough. Yes, that's good, Josh." She smiled.

Turning to the waiter, I repeated, "A *kruuu-sahnt,* please?"

"Yes, sir. A *croissant* for you," the waiter said with a polite smile, one that had quickly replaced the rude expression on his face.

"Thank you," I replied with a quiet sigh of relief.

In addition to having learned how to say that word properly, that was the first lunch where the true tradition began. We had lunches before that time, but this was the first lunch that I really talked to her as a friend and mentor. And that was the first lunch that she really dug deep and offered me advice, advice that proved to be useful as I entered the first year of my college experience at Gallaudet University.

In addition to advice, she and Uncle Robert, along with Grandma, had provided me invaluable sponsorship for events that would help further along my education and networking: providing a plane ticket here and there for my camping trips, providing a check to pay the difference (after the scholarships were applied) in the cost of my trip to Washington, DC as a part of the Close-Up Foundation program, and having been generous enough to give me odd jobs during the years before my sixteenth birthday.

Aunt Julie has also inspired an intense energy within me, an energy that comes outwards, allowing me to accomplish anything I've ever wanted; this became more and more apparent over the past few years. Others have nurtured my energy within, but Julie was the one who helped unlock that energy.

I see Aunt Julie as the J.Lo of the family; she has an energy that matches the Latina pop singer and the looks to match. Her determinedness also matches that of Jennifer Lopez.

She had always been very clear-cut about how she perceived things in this world; she never had worried about offending me in terms of telling me what I really needed to hear. She has always told me exactly the way she felt about many things. That kind of brutal honesty was unknowingly welcomed into my library. Aunt Julie stepped in when many people in my family and outside world were afraid to say anything that would have potentially upset me. She taught me that I should not wallow in self-pity, but to take control of the little things in my life.

I don't wish to discredit anybody in the family, of course not. They all have done the exactly same thing. But when you have a friend inside the family and that person tells you what you need to hear, you're more liable to accept it without prejudice, without offense. Maybe it's because she is such a good psychologist; indeed, she got her BA in psychology from the University of Oklahoma.

The bottom line is her way of handling things very frankly had helped inspire me to look at the world in a much more assertive way. Over the past few years, I've begun to stand up and say *no* to many things, things that seemed to work against me because of my Deafness.

She was one of the many people in my library that helped me solidify the concept that I can be assertive, yet not aggressive. Julie also showed me that I should state my desires and goals and follow through with them, that nobody will distract me from getting what I wanted in life.

———————————————

You know, Julie became even more important to me during my earliest years of college; with Mommy being newly married, I sought out a new friendship within the family. Certainly, it's odd that I would say something like this concerning Mommy, but she was my best friend until she married Dad. So it was natural that I looked for someone else, and that was where Aunt Julie came in.

She had unknowingly become my first mentor, a new additional role model in my life; she had obtained a college degree herself, and I looked to her for advice in how to handle things in life in terms of a college experience. And the way she handled things were different than mine. I wanted to understand how she was able to keep things simple and functional. After having been to Washington, DC via the excellent Close-Up Foundation in April of 1995, thanks to Julie and Robert, and having visited Gallaudet, I decided to enroll there for my university studies.

During my years there, Julie and I corresponded

through letters (this was before e-mail and the Internet became widely available to everybody in this world); those letters were always full of advice and philosophical discussions about things in life. It was a good thing for me because my years at Gallaudet University tested everything I knew and understood about the world in which I grew up; those years also taught me things that I never thought of.

There is also something else about Aunt Julie that everybody should know: she is a very giving and caring person. She seeks not the attention, but enjoys the affirmation that comes with giving. She is always there for you, whether it be that you need a ride or just someone to talk to. I know this is a rather short chapter on an important person in my life, but I've always seen my relationship with Julie as this: meaningful yet simple. To this day, we still enjoy our lunches. We still hang out, like friends would. We shop together, go to Starbucks, and often go to the beachside for lunch.

She was someone who stepped in and taught me that the simpler your life is, the happier you will be. She, along with Dad, helped me understand how simple and happy Josh could be. Only recently have I begun to look at that on many different levels.

Dear Julie,

I'm thankful to have you in my life. Not only are you my favorite aunt, but you've become the mentor that stands behind me as I face the world. You have helped me learn how to keep my light burning by keeping things clear and concise. You inspire me with your insightful perspective on how things work in life. Your simplicity inspires me. I only hope that I have appropriately described how important you are to me. Indeed, you have a very special place in my library for you have invested a considerable amount of time in my life.

I send you much love from my library!

Your nephew,
Josher

THE IVORY TOWER

Looking up to the bottom of the last floor as he exited the door of Julie, the master absentmindedly pulled the great old oak ladder from the trapdoor beneath him; he pulled it and placed it upon the rim of the trapdoor above him. The master was now ready to see what was behind that door, that very last door, a door that watched over the functions of the library behind a hidden shadow.

After having climbed onto the final, top floor of the entire library, the master saw that there still existed the heavy padlock, securing a blockade to the other side of the door. One could not open it without a specific key. With a sigh, the master fumbled through his pocket bag and attempted to locate the key ring; there had been many keys on the ring, and he wondered if he would be able to locate the right one. Pulling the ring out, the master tried every single key. None of them would fit the padlock hole.

Throwing the keys down and quickly becoming frustrated, the master kicked the padlock. He also tried to smash it with a nearby glass globe that had been hanging from the wall. The padlock resisted. There was no way in heaven or on earth that it would unlock. Cursing under his breath, the master sighed. How will he continue? How can he finish this chapter in his own life without this door?

Am I missing something? the master pondered. His forehead was pressed upon the cold, mysterious surface of the last door.

Suddenly, a flash of white-hot light fleeced the face of the master through a nearby window on the level; it had been coming from a distance in the forest. The light had somehow signaled itself to the master, who happened to be standing next to the small square window.

Squinting at the source of the sporadically flashing light, the master tried to identify the source to no avail. The background of the dark forest and the foothills did not hold any indication that there was life nor activity. Noticing a familiar telescope that had somehow appeared in a corner, the master grabbed the auxiliary lenses and peered through them. What the master saw surprises him, for the light was so beautiful.

"Wow. I nearly forgot all about that place!" the master whispered as his left eye fixated upon the image through the telescope: a majestic foundation against the backdrop of the greatest mountains in the world, an American flag rippling gently along the trade winds upon a small, Gothic chapel, an entire structure held by a strong, yet delicate tower of whiteness. And it stood out in the land where the end was never in sight.

The master's eye misted over as he looked at the most profound place that existed outside his library, a place he had annexed to his own library from a distance, a place where his consciousness was forever altered, a place where he understood himself better.

He smiled as he continued looking through the lenses. He was now looking at his second home: Gallaudet University, the ivory tower of the landscape inside the master's dreams.

It glistened under the midday sun, beckoning the master to return.

The glistening of the tower was only the beginning of a very long undergraduate career spanning a good eight years, constantly interrupted by life, and it had forever placed the master on a completely different level than ever before.

And it immediately brought back memories to the master.

August 1997

"Mom! Hurry up! I have to go! I can't miss my flight!" I said with a great deal of hysteria.

I had just looked at my flight time and realized I was an hour off.

It was August 1997, and I was packed and ready to fly off from Oklahoma City to Washington, DC for an experience that would prove to be a challenging one. I was only seventeen and had just gotten back from a relaxing summer in Florida, where my grandmother had relocated. I also had gotten out of the mental institution right before then; the summer had helped me put my problems away until they came back later to haunt me.

"Josh, okay. Christina, are you ready? We need to take him to the airport," Mom said with a stressed-out tone of voice.

We loaded into the car and rushed off to the airport. As soon as I checked in at the airport, I had to run to the airplane or else I'd miss it. Mommy, Christina, and I rushed to my gate and within what seemed to be a matter of minutes, I had hugged them quickly, posed for a photograph, and had located my seat on the plane. And then we pulled away from the gate.

That was it. And it would be a long time before I'd see them again. After seventeen years of having a son, Mommy was all of a sudden without one. She just had lost her son to the world. The image of a very sad, heartbroken Mommy standing alone with a young teenaged sister as I ran down the tarmac, looking back at them and waving hastily, burned in my mind.

August 1997
"Do you have everything you need, Josh?" a voice said.

"Do you need food?" another voice rang out.

"Are you warm enough? Do you need coffee?" yet another voice cut in.

"Some money, perhaps?"

The master was loading up his personal belongings. Mommy, Ken, Christina, Julie, and Grandma were outside in front of the library. A white horse stood ever so steadfast, waiting for the librarian to say his good-byes.

"I'm all right. Don't you worry; I'll be all right. Max will guide me. He has never steered me wrong before," the master said as he patted the proud horse. "He has a sense of direction that I could never understand."

"Okay," Mommy said quietly. Sighing, the master pulled out the antique golden key and handed it to his Mommy.

"Mommy, please watch over my library while I'm gone. You're the only one I can trust," he said as he closed his mother's hands around the golden, gilded key. He saw that his mother was about to cry. Not wanting to get emotional, he cut the conversation short.

"Well. I guess I'll see you soon. I need to go," the master said abruptly and got onto the back of his beloved horse.

"I love you, Josh. Please call me call when you get there, okay?" Mommy said.

"Okay, I will. Love you."

And with a swift kick to the horse's sides, the master shot off, running down the rich, lush green lawn of the library, across the running river, and disappeared within the shadows of the dark forest. Glancing back right before he disappeared into the forest, he could see the figure representing Mommy dropping to the floor, as if she were crying.

Sitting in a window seat, I watched nonchalantly as the barely visible landscape below me passed by; I was on my way to Chicago O'Hare where I was to change planes before arriving to my final destination. Excitement inside me could barely be contained. A new experience lay before me. And I was terrified. In Chicago, I sat down at a café and ate a bagel and a glass of milk before getting on the plane that was headed for Washington.

I had read virtually every piece of literature possible, literature that illustrated the significance of Gallaudet University within the Deaf world; I was dumbfounded to learn how so many Deaf people studied there. Indeed, my mind was constantly flying back to that day in April of 1995 when I visited Gallaudet for the first time.

Nothing was like it, the flux of students coming and going to the campus, the faculty and the staff conversing amongst themselves in sign language. I had never encountered such a situation before. My mind just could not comprehend it. Yet I could not wait to embrace a new experience, an experience that the small rural communities and suburbs of Oklahoma could never offer me.

My eyes closed and I drifted off to a light sleep as I flew from Chicago to Washington, D.C.

"Here, Max. Here's some sugar cubes," the master said to his white mustang. The horse munched on them, as if they were a well-deserved reward. And they were.

The librarian and the horse were exhausted from the first leg of the journey. It was twilight, and they were to camp out for the night. They had stopped at a halfway point, one that went beyond the forest and found itself at the foothills of the mountains; those mountains had to be conquered first before he could see the full vestige of the ivory tower.

Along the route, the master could see the glistening dome of the structure on the very top of the tower. That flag and that small chapel seemed to beckon to the master's heart. The master and Max had rushed through the forest with an amazing speed; he could not wait to get there. Far, yet so close was the ivory tower.

The master knew they would have to get going again, because only a light sleep was all the master could afford at that time. He wanted to get there as soon as possible. He drifted into sleep for a few hours.

"Go, Max! Go, run!" the master hollered after their brief break. The horse ran so fast that the master had a hard time holding onto it. They were headed dead for the Ivory Tower.

A blink of an eye later, they arrived.

Panting, the horse tottered to a halt. The master jumped off the horse.

He couldn't believe how beautiful the walls of the ivory tower were. It was as if he were looking at a wall of pearl and ivory. Nothing in his whole life had looked so shiny or pure.

There was a small coffin-shaped, golden door directly in front of him; a security guard stood there with a kind smile.

"Name? Purpose of visit?" the guard inquired.

"I'm Joshua Dowling. I've come from the rivers and plains far away. I've come for my education," the master replied.

"No need to speak with your voice. You can use sign language. You will always be understood here. Gallaudet will never turn you away. You are welcome to enter," the guard signed to the master, and he opened the golden coffin door that led to the stairs.

The guard smiled and winked. "I will take care of your horse. Fret not, for he will be well fed and well sheltered. Go. They are waiting for you. They are expecting you, sir."

"Thank you," the master signed.

And he disappeared behind the golden door, where he would take the stairs that led the master to the fabled land of Kendall Green, into a land that he had never seen or experienced, a land where the most unique people existed, worked, and lived.

"Welcome to Washington, DC. The current temperature is ninety-four degrees, and it is very humid out there," the flight attendant boomed in the microphone. With a smile, she added, "Thank you for flying Delta Airlines, and we wish you a pleasant day."

I had just landed into Washington, DC at the Reagan National Airport. I've arrived. I did it. My dream came true. I was going to college. I couldn't believe it. After having taken a cab and the trip down through the streets of Washington, DC, the cab driver pulled up to a small, yet elegantly gated campus on 800 Florida Avenue, N.E. I rolled down the window and stuck my head out like some kind of campy tourist. I looked at the security officer and was unsure if I should speak or sign.

"Hi! Is this Gallaudet University?" I inquired with an exuberant tone of voice, coupled with an exciting series of signed words. I was halfway through the window of the back seat of the cab. I also thrust the registration card toward him, nearly slamming him in the face while he had bowed down to meet my face.

Slightly surprised at my energy, he replied in sign language, "Yes. Welcome to Gallaudet! You need to go this way." He demonstrated the direction with his index finger, smiling at the same time. The direction was pointed toward the Field House, where all the P.E. classes were held, and it was also where the new freshmen registration and orientation took place.

"Thank you! Thank you so much!" I said. "Go! Yes, that way. No, no! *That* way, sir!" I squealed at the cab driver, as he almost went the opposite direction.

After getting out of the taxicab and paying the confused driver, I took my carry-on bag (my luggage were still missing, presumably somewhere in Chicago, and I only had my book-bag. This resulted in me going without my underwear and clothes for an entire week. I thank my college roommate who had helped me out in that situation) and marched right into Field House. My energy was all over the place. I couldn't wait to see what Gallaudet had to offer.

"Hi! Welcome to Gallaudet! It's so good to see you again!" one of the recruiters said to me after seeing me rush in like some kind of speed demon. She had come to Oklahoma as a recruiter and had successfully done a good job in explaining to me the incredible benefits of this fine university. Her smile was truly infectious, and I could see in her eyes a person who was overjoyed to see me at Gallaudet. And she had, up to that point, known how to talk to me; for some reason, she had a calming effect on me and helped orient myself around a completely alien (albeit fascinating) landscape.

"Hi! Hi!" I said with a slightly overwhelmed and confused tone in sign language. Smiling, she led me to the line where I would go through the usual round of stuff that came with being a new college student. She kept tabs on me until the time I was taken to my first dorm room.

And thus began my Gallaudet experience.

You know what? I could very easily create an entire book, a body of work representing the infinite nuances that exist in the Deaf world. I would love to go into great detail how every single element had affected me.

But for the sake of this current autobiography, I will concisely summarize major milestones at Gallaudet that have shaped my perception.

The first major thing is all too obvious: the fact that there was an actual liberal arts university geared exclusively toward members of the Deaf community, members that are hard-of-hearing or Deaf. Only recently has Gallaudet begun to open its doors for hearing students into its undergraduate programs (hearing students are accepted into the graduate programs, and it has been that way for a long time). This illustrates the desire on the university's part to encompass a more broad understanding of how its role works in a particular community, be it Deaf or hearing. For me, the role of Gallaudet had affected a larger understanding of how the Deaf culture had flourished over hundreds of years; indeed, it was the first time I actually learned the relatively unspoken history of the Deaf people and how they had played a fundamental role in several aspects of society as we now know it.

With that first milestone, I saw it was, as JoJo had told me many years before, indeed possible to be Deaf, proud, happy, fulfilled, and well-socialized. If only I had known that anytime sooner in my life.

The second thing that struck me about Gallaudet was the ability to be educated in any subject matter, in any specific major that you wanted to pursue. I would like, right now, to take the opportunity to extend my heartfelt thanks to the Department of Foreign Literature, Languages, and Cultures at Gallaudet. Without them, I would not have had a much deeper understanding of how important foreign languages are. I finally understood how important it was that a person be well aware of the countries outside our backyard, to be acutely capable of communicating with others in different tongues or sign languages.

For me, the faculty, staff, and students in the department had unknowingly changed many things in my life, in areas of classroom interactions, formal language instruction, ways of handling the stresses that a new college student is not accustomed to, and providing an abundance of personal advice. The members of the department had always taken a very serious interest in how well I would do, and they never cut me any slack when it came to the level of performance expected from me. Once again, I was blessed with the continuation of good quality education that I left behind in Oklahoma there at Kendall Green.

Even more so, I give additional thanks to both the Honors department and the English department. Without them, I would have not been able to pursue a rigorous curriculum, one designed to challenge your thoughts and your writing skills. I stress that if it had not been for these departments, it would have proved me an almost impossible task to write this story. One more department I wish to recognize is the First Year Seminar (FYS) department. Without the guidance of the staff members and professors there, I would have not as quickly assumed control of my academic future had they been absent from my college experience.

Yes, I had all the problems previously mentioned that worked against me, but with the support of all these departments, I was able to somewhat assume control, and it still carries on to this day. In addition to writing, I was able to approach that most dreaded subject of my entire academic sphere: math.

Far be it from me to understand the purpose of an algebraic expression, a postulate, a theorem, or even a statistical data table. To this day, the area of mathematics and geometry throws me into a state of anxiety. With the support of the Tutorial Center and countless peers, I was able to overcome that. And I made no less than a C+ on all my math classes, fortunately. But I had to work very hard.

The point here, ladies and gentlemen, is that we all have something that we are terrible at, academically speaking. I could learn ten languages and be fluent in them by the day I die, but I still cannot perform a complicated equation without resorting to external notes and references.

If you feel that you are overwhelmed with your first years as a college student, especially if you are a student at Gallaudet, never forget the opportunities for improvement, for Gallaudet never falls short of its promise to service you in the best way possible (or at any university that you might attend, naturally).

There is that next milestone that occurred during my latter years as a college student there (after 2003, when I took five years off to do some exploring within my heart): overcoming the idea of racism and prejudice. This may strike the reader as a little bit off the point, but this cannot be ignored. I have never been comfortable about any type of discussion when it came to the idea of racism. Until then, I had no idea that I harbored some type of racism. Not to say it was openly hostile racism or anything, but there existed that small grain of prejudice, for I hail from what people call "White Bread America." Coming to Washington, DC, where the population is overwhelmingly African-American in terms of demographics, I saw how different my world was back home; indeed, the adjustment proved to be a big shock it was for me.

How funny. Me, a Deaf person who knows struggles on a daily basis; yet I couldn't extend that understanding to someone of a different racial class. This proves that racism is a very serious problem in this country, one that transcends all different groups of people. And it does affect the Deaf community, too. I am glad to say today that I no longer have any negative perspectives on the people of color in this country. I used to grant only certain exceptions (Oprah, Tyra Banks, etc.), but I now view everybody who is of color as individuals with their own contributions to society. I recognize that I'm a human, and I get scared of anything that seems different, but I am not one to judge.

We all are not that different in terms of race, social class, and whatnot, when you think about it.

Indeed, with the election of Obama and the fact that he and his family are the first African-American family to employ the White House, it only gives more reason for us Americans to be open minded to diversity. Change shall be embraced, for without change, we both as individuals and as a nation, would continue to stagnate and not grow.

Thank you, Professor, the one that taught that course in racial diversity. It really changed many things for me, for so much the better! I owe you big time, for you had showed me that being aware, respectful and kind to a specific group of people would help you be the same to everybody in general. You taught me what it was like being a human and how I could exhort myself to bring out the positivism within me and allow others to see that. It was a truly unique learning experience. I only hope I have expressed this eloquently enough for you, Professor.

One other major thing that I learned from Gallaudet (certainly, there will be many more things that the university will continue to impart in me in the years to come): the concept of proper self-conduct and how you present yourself to the outside world, in addition to being well-versed in the social circles.

Certainly, I never had a problem in the hearing world. I was able to fool quite a few people, putting on that "poor Deaf me" act and getting what I wanted. But not at Gallaudet. As I had previously mentioned in chapter 3, the Deaf card was constantly declined; it was not accepted anywhere on Kendall Green.

So, for the first time, I couldn't hide, not even from myself. That, of course, led to some problems, but with the greater understanding I have of myself now, I'm glad to say that my ability to be more sociable is credited to Gallaudet University.

I'm going to just close this chapter with a simple thought, simple yet profound: As the years pass, Gallaudet will always remain my one and only Ivory Tower, a gleaming example of near-perfect Deaf utopia (despite that it, like every university in this country and overseas, has its own unique struggles), in the ever-changing landscape that I call the outside world, a world that continues to be a part of my never-ending story.

Thank you, Gallaudet, for letting me enter and being a part of your world. The longer I keep you in my life, the more I can't imagine my life without you. There will be scores and scores of written works (I hope!) in the future that will continue to include you, my personal ivory tower, which will show the world just how significant you are in our world, both Deaf and hearing.

You, this small, humble Deaf university on 800 Florida Avenue, NE, have forever completed my identity as a Deaf person.

More importantly, you taught me how to love myself.

THE LAST DOOR

The master sighed as he stepped back from the telescope and looked at the gleaming ivory tower through the window, tiny in the far distance yet so significant; he began to think about his experiences, both happy and sad, that had made up such a rich tapestry of his life. That tapestry, with its intricate embroidery and colorful illustrations depicting the greatest epic battles of Joshua with himself and the world, became very clear in the master's mind. The experiences. The lessons. The uneasy journey toward that elusive idea of knowing oneself. It was all a part of a big plan.

The master now understood. He understood that every single event had a profound impact on him and that they all were equally important. To take one of the loose threads out of the richly woven tapestry would be to unravel the entire piece of fabric. No matter what had happened, everything had become a contribution to create the reality and life of the librarian. He has now truly understood; he now finally got it, the whole deal. But, still, something was missing, that X factor, that certain thing that you couldn't put a finger on. A thread was missing from the tapestry. And it needed to be found.

The padlock unlocked itself. And it fell from the door.

The loud crash of the heavy, iron padlock shook the library; the sound of the padlock falling upon the floor reverberated throughout the entire library, and the master screamed at the sound, for he had been standing right next to the door. The bundle of heavy chains escaped the handle of the last door and piled upon the padlock, covering it. Slowly, the door swung wide open.

The master stood in front of the entrance to the mysterious last door for a great deal of time; he had no idea what to expect, the things inside. He had spent a great deal of time investigating every single room, save this one. What joys would he find in there? What horrors would he find in there? What situations or ideas were in this room?

How would he even know? He doesn't even know what this door was for. It was always this well-veiled door that he never gave much thought to. It was always the part of his life that he couldn't figure out. It had been blocked from the master; he couldn't get into it if he had tried as hard as he could. Nonetheless, the master felt a sense of calm and serenity. He wasn't so afraid of this room. There was something about that space, a space that seemed to draw him in.

Upon entering the room, the master noticed that there existed virtually nothing inside, save a small twin-sized bed and an entire wall made of windows. Indeed, those windows were not covered by the all-too-familiar black velvet drapes that had been present in all of the previous rooms.

The master noticed something near the bed that had been positioned right along one of the big windows.

A small boy, about eight years of age, was kneeled on the floor, his arms propped upon the mattress of the bed. His hands were clasped together, and the boy was praying.

"Please … please. . . ." The words accompanied some mumbling words that escaped the young boy's mouth. The boy had a familiar accent, an accent that the master had heard somewhere else a long time ago. As the master stood there, he noticed that the boy's face was laden with tears, accompanied by puffy-red eyes. He was crying as he prayed; indeed, his small, fragile frame shook with each sob. And the boy kept looking up to the window, looking at the stars and the full moon that was present outside the library.

A carefully folded note sat on the mattress next to the boy. The boy took the note and held it out to the window and cried.

"Please. Where are you? I need you. What did I do wrong?" the boy sobbed, the note shaking with each sob that quivered from the boy's heart. The master immediately recognized the boy.

He was looking at himself, a younger version of a boy who had begun to understand the cruel reality of the world, a boy whose heart was ripped into shreds as he realized that his wish would never come true, a wish that remained still in the master's heart. With a sad heart, the master walked over to the little boy. The boy couldn't see the master, but the master could. How evident the pain was on the boy's face. That young face that only had begun to understand what rejection was.

What disappointments lay out in front of him. What a cold world it was out there.

The master kneeled down to the eye level of the little boy and stared at the young one. A nice, handsome face was twisted with agony and pain, and there seemed to be no ending in sight for his deep pain, a pain that would forever be burned into his eyes and soul. The master only knew too well that pain, the pain that he had only recently begun to overcome.

Suppressing the urge to cry, the master stood up, took a deep breath, and turned to the great Tudor windows of the room. He looked out to the sky through the detailed glass. He saw how beautiful the night sky was with its twinkling stars and the full, monolithic moon. The master folded his arms together to keep himself warm and sighed. He then opened his mouth.

"Can someone come and help this boy? I don't want him to end up like me. Someone spare him please," the master spoke out to the evening air to nobody in particular, a hint of desperation in his voice.

Then it happened.

Behind the master, a source of light became alive. It began as a small pin-sized ball of light, and it gradually became bigger and bigger; slowly, but surely, the shimmering blue ball of light lit up the entire room. And the room became warm from the beautiful light. Noticing and feeling the light radiating behind him, the master turned around slowly. And found himself face to face with the person he had been looking for all his life.

The Blue Fairy.

Over twenty years after that first note I wrote during a cold, wintry night of December 4, 1987, the Blue Fairy had finally come. She had finally answered my prayers and my cries for help. *She came.*

Musical notes from a piano in the background tickled the room's air like soap bubbles. Warmth surrounded the room like a cloak of cinnamon. Peace ruled the room like an invisible force. The blue light radiated from Blue Fairy.

The Blue Fairy herself was sheathed in a light, pale-blue chiffon dress, a fabric that seemed to shimmer and flutter with the gentle warm breeze; her complexion was fair and clear, and her chestnut-brown hair accentuated her deep, clear blue eyes. A smile rested upon her face like one of the greatest models of Leonardo da Vinci, subtle yet profound. Her stance was firm, yet gentle and kind. The silver wand in her hand moved around gracefully as she extended her arms toward the master; her movements were very slow and dreamlike. In front of the master, stood the epitome of serenity, peace, and happiness.

"I can't believe it. You came. Where were you when I needed you?" the master blurted out almost impolitely, a tone that carried a mixture of shock, happiness, and indignation.

The Blue Fairy only looked with a smile. Her right hand held the wand as she extended out her left hand, which held something. The master, noticing this, reached out and took the concealed object out of her hand. It was a bundle of papers. The master undid the red, scarlet ribbon that had held the papers together. Immediately, he recognized one of the papers. He couldn't forget the handwriting if he had tried:

Dear Blue Fairy,

My name is Josh. I read about you in the book.
You are so pretty and nice ... ...

With a gaping facial expression that showed shock and awe, the master looked quickly up to the fairy. He was holding the letters with a shaky hand. It took him a minute or two to articulate his thoughts.

"What ... this is mine. I wrote this! But ... but how did—" the master exclaimed. His eyes burned into the fairy's, searching and wanting answers. The Blue Fairy softly cut him short.

"Dearest Josh, how I wish to help you understand. What you hold in your hand are the words of your heart. You have spoken to me for many, many years. For over twenty years I have stood by you as you meandered through your life. For years I watched a young boy with a beautiful, but hidden warm heart grow to become the man that stands before me. Dearest Josh, the truth is this: I came to you the very first time you called out to me. I came and I stayed. And I never left you," she said with an air of gentleness and wisdom.

"But I don't understand. I mean, I don't understand. If you say you were with me this whole time, how come I didn't see you or at least felt something? You could have at least given me a sign!" the master said.

"It is not how it is done, for you could never have been able to see me until you understood yourself. My dearest child, I spoke to you through your heart. I guided you and shielded you from dangerous situations. I made sure doors were opened for you. I protected you and guided you. There were many, many signs out there. And you recognized them. You only did not realize it," the Blue Fairy said. "Think back to that day. You asked me if I could repair your wooden ears. Do you remember the request you had made?"

"Yes. Why am I still Deaf?" the master blurted out. He was becoming quite upset, yet in awe of what she was telling him.

"Don't you see, Josh? The first and the last day you wrote to me, you asked twice that I fix your wooden ears. There is nothing wrong with your ears. It is not your ears that I fixed, youngest Joshua. It is not your ears that prevented you from succeeding in life. It was your heart that I fixed today. For years I've watched you turn that sweet, soft heart into hard wood, and when the time was right, I was asked by God to fix your heart so that you could learn how to be loved and to love others," the Blue Fairy said as her kind eyes gazed upon the master's tear-drenched face. She continued, "Please tell me, young Josh, what you think this means." Unable to stand any longer, the master sat on the floor with a pensive look on his face.

"Well, I guess you are maybe telling me that not being able to hear isn't really a disability after all. Maybe it was my heart and mind that created a disability for myself," he began.

"Yes. Very good, continue," the Blue Fairy said with a smile.

"Um, well, maybe I made my heart a wooden one by building a wall around me. Like, I didn't want to let people in. Like, I was afraid of life. And I became cold and mean. Thinking it's my Deafness that blocked me from doing what I hoped to do, but the whole time, it's really my attitude and my heart that had prevented me from doing so … And that I had to figure it out for myself. Am I right?" the librarian asked with an expected look on his face.

"Yes. And not only that, but you've been able to do that with my help. I helped you find a way to unlock that heart. People love you, young Josh. They want nothing but the best things for you. But you have to want it too. You cannot achieve something without having the desire for it. You see, I never left you. How could I?" the Blue Fairy ended.

She approached the master and opened her arms; the master, still slightly confused at the events that were unfolding, went up to her. With a slightly guarded stance, he allowed the Blue Fairy to hug him. As he felt the warm embrace of the fairy around his shoulders and back, he broke down. The feeling was wonderful, yet it hurt more than anything he could have ever imagined. Sobbing happily, he hugged the Blue Fairy tightly, and whispered, "Thank you for never leaving me."

And as soon as those words escaped his lips, the Blue Fairy's wand touched the top of his head, and a wave of shimmering light surrounded him, just like it had surrounded the puppet in the Disney movie. And the fairy released young Joshua and floated out of the great Tudor windows of the room, taking the ball of light with her.

As she left, these words filled the room, "Dearest Josh, please know this. I will never leave you. You will always have me, whether or not you see me. Just wish on the biggest star in the night sky, and I will always help you remember the goodness within you. Josh, go. It is time for you to be the leader you were meant to be. It is your time now. You are now ready."

And as the last word languished in the room, she disappeared. The master was now left alone in the darkness. But it was all right. His heart was finally free of the wooden splinters that had plagued him for years. His wish had come true after all these years. The weight of the entire world had been lifted off his shoulders. Joshua was now, for the first time in his entire life, happy. As the master left the room with a relaxed comportment, he looked over to the corner where the bed and the boy were. What he saw was something he had been desperately seeking all these years: peace.

Indeed, right under the beautiful stained glass Tudor windows along the wall, the little boy, for the first time in a long time, was sleeping soundly on his bed with a teddy bear tucked underneath his arms.

With the moonlight beams dancing on his face, young Joshua was sleeping as if he had never slept before.